Clubs, churches, unions, societies . . .

All organizations require a manual of standard procedure, and ROBERT'S RULES OF ORDER has provided the classic principles for more than a century. Now, this new, revised, and updated edition will teach anyone, even beginners, the essential rules of procedure, including . . .

* An orderly method of running meetings — smoothly and fairly

* Nominations and elections

* Secretary's minutes

* Treasurer's reports

* Bylaws and resolutions

* Amendments

* And much more . . .

Robert's Rules of Order
The Modern Edition

THE MODERN EDITION

ROBERT'S RULES OF ORDER

Original 1876 Edition by Major Henry M. Robert
Completely Revised by Darwin Patnode, Ph.D.

B
BERKLEY BOOKS, NEW YORK

This Berkley book contains the complete text
of the original hardcover edition.

ROBERT'S RULES OF ORDER
MODERN EDITION

A Berkley Book / published by arrangement with
Barbour & Company, Inc.

PRINTING HISTORY
Thomas Nelson edition published 1989
Berkley edition / August 1989

The Penguin Putnam Inc. World Wide Web site address is
http://www.penguinputnam.com

ISBN: 0-425-11690-5

BERKLEY®
Berkley Books are published by
The Berkley Publishing Group, a division of Penguin Putnam Inc.,
375 Hudson Street, New York, New York 10014.
BERKLEY and the "B" design are trademarks
belonging to Penguin Putnam Inc.

PRINTED IN THE UNITED STATES OF AMERICA

25   24   23   22   21   20   19   18

CONTENTS

COMPENDIUM OF RULES ON MOTIONS

Part 1—Order of Precedence of Motions

Adjourn
Recess
Raise a question of privilege
Call for the orders of the day
Lay on the table
Order the previous question (close debate)
Limit or extend limits of debate
Postpone definitely
Commit or refer
Amend
Postpone indefinitely
Main motion

These twelve motions have a fixed rank, called the order of precedence, among themselves. When one of them is pending, any motion higher on the list is permitted, with a few rare exceptions specified in the text, and any motion lower on the list is prohibited, except that to amend or to order the previous question on *an amendable higher-ranking motion* is permitted when the higher-ranking motion is pending. They are proposed in any upward sequence and put to vote in the opposite downward sequence.

Part 2—Six Basic Facts about Each Motion

This table gives six basic facts about each motion. The motions are in alphabetical order by their key words. Because no table can include all exceptions and variations, the reader should study the text before using this table as a quick reference; two-thirds votes, for instance, *are especially likely to have important qualifications given in the text*. The abbreviations are the following: Anoth = is in order when another person has the floor; Sec = requires a second; Deb = is debatable; Amd = is amendable; Maj = requires a majority vote; $2/3$ = requires a two-thirds vote; C = is decided by the chair; Auto = is automatic upon demand; Rec = is reconsiderable; A = only if affirmative; N = only if negative. A minus sign (−) means NOT. Thus, −Deb means NOT DEBATABLE; ReconA means RECONSIDERABLE ONLY IF THE VOTE WAS AFFIRMATIVE.

Adjourn (when privileged)	−Anoth Sec −Deb Amd Maj −Rec
Agenda, adopt an	−Anoth Sec Deb Amd Maj RecN
Agenda, amend an adopted	−Anoth Sec Deb Amd $2/3$ RecN
Agenda, suspend the	−Anoth Sec −Deb −Amd $2/3$ −Rec
Amend a pending motion	−Anoth Sec Deb Amd Maj Rec
Amend after adoption	−Anoth Sec Deb Amd $2/3$ RecN
Appeal (general case)	Anoth Sec Deb −Amd Maj Rec
Appeal (exceptional case)	Anoth Sec −Deb −Amd Maj Rec
Blank, create a	−Anoth Sec −Deb −Amd Maj −Rec
Blank, fill a	−Anoth −Sec Deb −Amd Maj Rec
Bylaws, adopt original	−Anoth Sec Deb Amd Maj RecN
Bylaws, amend adopted	−Anoth Sec Deb Amd $2/3$ RecN
Commit	−Anoth Sec Deb Amd Maj Rec

Committee, discharge a	—Anoth Sec Deb Amd Maj RecN
Committee of the whole, go into	—Anoth Sec Deb Amd Maj Rec
Consider informally	—Anoth Sec Deb – Amd Maj RecN
Debate, close	—Anoth Sec –Deb – Amd 2/3 Rec
Debate, limit or extend limits of	—Anoth Sec –Deb Amd 2/3 Rec
Divide the assembly	Anoth –Sec –Deb Amd Auto –Rec
Divide the motion (on demand)	Anoth –Sec –Deb – Amd Auto –Rec
Divide the motion (not on demand)	—Anoth Sec –Deb Amd Maj –Rec
Executive session, go into	—Anoth Sec Deb Amd Maj Rec
MAIN MOTION OR QUESTION	—Anoth Sec Deb Amd Maj Rec
Minority views, receive	—Anoth Sec –Deb Amd Maj Rec
Minutes, approve or correct pending	—Anoth Sec Deb Amd Maj Rec
Minutes, approve without reading	—Anoth Sec Deb Amd Maj Rec
Minutes, dispense with reading the	—Anoth Sec –Deb – Amd 2/3 –Rec
Nominate	—Anoth Sec –Deb – Amd Maj –Rec
Nominations, adopt motions related to	—Anoth –Sec Deb – Amd Maj –Rec
Nominations, close	—Anoth Sec –Deb Amd Maj Rec
Nominations, reopen	—Anoth Sec –Deb Amd 2/3 – Rec
Object to consideration	—Anoth Sec –Deb Amd Maj RecN
Order of business, adopt an	Anoth –Sec –Deb – Amd 2/3 RecN
Orders of the day, call for the	—Anoth Sec Deb Amd 2/3 RecN
Orders of the day, make general	Anoth –Sec –Deb – Amd Auto –Rec
Orders of the day, make special	Anoth Sec Deb Amd Maj Rec
Papers, giving permission to read	Anoth Sec Deb Amd 2/3 Rec
	Anoth –Sec –Deb – Amd Maj Rec

Parliamentary inquiry, make a	Anoth −Sec −Deb −Amd C −Rec
Point of order	Anoth −Sec −Deb −Amd C −Rec
Postpone definitely	−Anoth Sec Deb Amd Maj Rec
Postpone indefinitely	−Anoth Sec Deb −Amd Maj RecA
Previous question, order the	Anoth −Sec −Deb −Amd ⅔ Rec
Question of privilege, raise a	Anoth −Sec −Deb −Amd C −Rec
Question of privilege, adopt a	−Anoth Sec Deb Amd Maj Rec
Recess (when privileged)	−Anoth Sec −Deb Amd Maj −Rec
Reconsider a debatable motion	Anoth Sec Deb −Amd Maj Rec
Reconsider an undebatable motion	Anoth Sec −Deb −Amd Maj Rec
Refer	−Anoth Sec Deb Amd Maj Rec
Report, adopt or approve a	−Anoth Sec Deb Amd Maj Rec
Rescind or repeal	−Anoth Sec Deb Amd ⅔ RecN
Resolution, adopt or approve a	−Anoth Sec Deb Amd Maj Rec
Rules of order, suspend special/other	−Anoth Sec −Deb −Amd ⅔ −Rec
Rules of order, adopt special	−Anoth Sec Deb Amd ⅔ RecN
Rules of order, amend adopted special	−Anoth Sec Deb Amd ⅔ RecN
Standing rules, adopt	−Anoth Sec Deb Amd Maj Rec
Standing rules, amend adopted	−Anoth Sec Deb Amd ⅔ RecN
Standing rules, suspend	−Anoth Sec −Deb −Amd Maj −Rec
Table, lay on/take from the	−Anoth Sec −Deb −Amd Maj −Rec
Time, set the effective	−Anoth Sec Deb Amd Maj Rec
Voting, adopt motions related to	−Anoth Sec −Deb Amd Maj Rec
Withdraw a motion, give permission to	Anoth −Sec −Deb −Amd Maj RecN

11

PREFACE

Parliamentary law. Parliamentary law refers originally to the customs and rules of conducting business in the English Parliament and secondarily to the customs and rules of American legislative bodies. Because Americans do not have the respect the English have for customs, they tend to rely heavily, perhaps exclusively, on rules, which they usually prefer to have in writing. The United States Constitution—probably the best example of having rules and having them in writing—provides that each of the two houses of the national legislature may adopt its own rules of procedure, and they did so in their earliest days.

Those rules, however, were never intended to have any application beyond the legislative assemblies for which they were devised; thus, nonlegislative assemblies imitated them at their own risk. Furthermore, such imitations were not consistent from one organization to another, so a new member never knew quite what to expect.

The vast number of such groups—political, literary, scientific, benevolent, and religious—formed all over the United States still required some system of conducting their deliberations, and the nineteenth-century American obsession with efficiency dictated they be as uniform as feasible from one group to another.

For that reason, Henry M. Robert researched the rules of Congress, especially those of the House of Representatives, and other materials—including an 1845 book known as *Cushing's Manual*—concerning the rules of non-legislative assemblies.

He then devised and put in writing, in 1876, a set of rules for use in nonlegislative assemblies throughout the country. Robert, a military engineer with a religious background, said the object of his book was "to assist an assembly to accomplish the work for which it was designed, in the best possible manner. To do this it is necessary to restrain the individual somewhat, as the right of an individual in any community, to do what he pleases, is incompatible with the interests of the whole. Where there is no law, but every man does what is right in his own eyes, there is the least of real liberty. Experience has shown the importance of definiteness in the law; and in this country, where customs are so slightly established and the published manuals of parliamentary practice so conflicting, no society should attempt to conduct business without having adopted some work upon the subject, as the authority in all cases not covered by their own special rules."

Robert paid for the publication of his manual, and the publisher placed on the cover of the small volume the words *Robert's Rules of Order*. Robert wrote in his preface that a work on parliamentary law had long been needed, based in its general principles upon the rules of Congress, but adapted in its specifics to the use of ordinary societies. Such a work would give not only the methods of organizing and conducting meetings, the duties of officers, and the documents of an organization, but also the rules governing motions, including their forms, objects, characteristics, and other details. Robert supplemented his text with a useful "Table of Rules Relating to Motions" at the beginning of the book, enabling the presiding officer of a meeting to decide many parliamentary questions by a quick reference, without turning a page or using an index, and that feature was especially popular with readers. He included numerous footnotes concerning legislative procedure, and he wrote a lengthy introduction dealing with legislative procedure, but the goal of the text proper was to provide firm and uniform rules of order for deliberative assemblies throughout the land.

He succeeded. The book was extremely popular, and he continued from a time shortly after the first printing to the end of his long life to make countless modifications from one printing to the next. He inserted new rules and sometimes even reversed earlier rules. After several years he issued a completely new book, *Robert's Rules of Order Revised*. He also produced an elementary textbook, *Parliamentary Practice,* and a somewhat scholarly work, *Parliamentary Law*.

About this edition. Robert's original edition was successful but not perfect, as his own eagerness to make changes in it makes abundantly clear. The present edition tries to retain the best of the original style and content of Robert's ideas and supplement them with modern language and rules, seeking a golden mean. In most sections, the opening material is that of Robert, and gradually additional material merges with it.

Some specifics may be of interest to the reader. Where footnotes (most of which concerned legislative procedure) were obsolete, they have been eliminated; where they were not, they have been incorporated smoothly into the text. Innumerable and maddening cross-references have been removed, and several definitions of terms Robert assumed the reader knew have been inserted, either below or at their first appearance in the text (or both). Spelling, punctuation, and typography have been modernized. The table of motions has been improved dramatically, and in some cases the arrangement of the material in the text has been altered slightly to have a more logical sequence, especially for a beginner. Particularly troublesome, for instance, was the fact that Robert's first book covered many of its topics twice, once near the beginning and once near the end, often with only imperfect consistency, often without thoroughness. A reader had to consult two sections on almost every topic. Robert did not aim his book at beginners, and he advised them to read the second part before the first! All the important information from the second part has been transferred to earlier sections. A few paragraphs on new topics have been inserted (including the motion to rescind, which Robert added in a later printing), references to an obscure kind of adjournment motion have been deleted, and obscure points have been clarified. Robert's awkward syntax has been reworked. Sample bylaws have been inserted, as have longer sample minutes, and much of his unimportant introductory material has been omitted. Also, more attention has been given to the participation of women in meetings.

Yes, in some cases, the rules have been changed, and such changes simply follow the lead Robert signaled in his later parliamentary writings. Robert himself quoted "one of the greatest of English writers on parliamentary law" to the effect that it is most important simply to have a rule: "Whether these forms be in all cases the most rational or not is really not of so great importance. It is much more material that there should be a rule to go by, than what that rule is, that there may be a uniformity of proceeding in business, not subject to the caprice of the chairman, or captiousness of the members. It is very material that order, decency and regularity be preserved."

Thus, when an organization's bylaws designate as parliamentary authority *Robert's Rules of Order* without specifying an edition, there can easily be disagreement as to what a particular rule says, not only because several different printings contain somewhat different rules, but also because Robert was not always perfectly clear or consistent within a given printing. An organization wishing to follow the spirit of the original rules of Henry M. Robert but needing a definitive printing for reference would do well to adopt as its parliamentary authority the Modern Edition of *Robert's Rules of Order*.

Learning more. Parliamentary law is a complex subject, despite the fact this volume may appear slender and simple. A comprehensive knowledge of it requires study—almost memorization—of dozens of books as well as practical experience and an understanding of principles. This book is a basic reference book but does not claim to be comprehensive. For most organizations and for most meetings, it will prove very adequate. A parliamentarian is a person especially skilled in knowing and practicing parliamentary law. Most of the parliamentarian's time is spent advising the presiding officer, although the parliamentarian should certainly be accessible to others. Some groups prefer to designate one of their own members as a parliamentarian to advise on difficult points, and such a practice is often adequate, although a parliamentarian should both appear and be impartial.

For a group plagued by internal strife or external challenges or for an especially important meeting, such as an annual meeting or a meeting involving revision of bylaws, the expertise of a professional parliamentarian is necessary to interpret this book in light of the other writings of Henry M. Robert, as well as other factors in parliamentary law. To obtain the services of a professional parliamentarian, an organization should contact the American Institute of Parliamentarians or the National Association of Parliamentarians (addresses are available in a local library) or write to me in care of the publisher of this book. Professional parliamentarians serve organizations for a fee, and they both function in meetings and offer instruction in parliamentary law to presiding officers and members.

In cases where legal expertise is sought, the services of a competent attorney are necessary, but very few attorneys have credentials in parliamentary law, and the organization should not seek to obtain both skills in one person.

Principles. Parliamentary law rests on certain principles. Perhaps the most important is the principle of rights: the right of the majority ultimately to rule, the right of the minority to be heard, and the right of the individual to participate in the decision-making process. The principle of one thing at a time pervades parliamentary rules, though it recognizes some things may justifiably temporarily interrupt other things. This principle developed certain rules regarding germaneness of amendments and speeches, division of motions, and other matters. The principle of balance between affirmative and negative finds embodiment in various rules, including those pertaining to alternating speeches between pro and con as well as those requiring that both the affirmative and the negative vote be taken on all motions. Perhaps underlying all rules is a sense of parliamentary courtesy: one must debate measures, not members. Thus, speakers in a meeting treat one another with the finest decencies of society. Decorum is understood.

Sometimes these principles conflict and always they are abstract, so the purpose of rules is to strike a procedural balance that considers all the principles and enunciates a specific process by which those principles interact and work. In other words, rules are representatives of the principles, both to give specific guidance on method and to provide a reasonable compromise in the event of conflict.

Regardless of one person's perception of the principles, the rules must be allowed to govern. These principles, though noble and right, do not offer the specificity meetings require; as a result, there may be disagreement about their application. For that reason, members of organizations agree to follow specific rules set forth in a book such as this, and in parliamentary law as in other law, the specific takes priority over the general. Thus, members cannot claim that the rules in this manual do not apply in a given case just because they seem, to their interests, to violate the general principles of parliamentary law. Those general principles are transcendent, but *these rules rule*.

Definitions. Before reading further, the student of parliamentary law should study carefully the following definitions, because these terms occur often in the text, have precise and somewhat technical meanings that can be decisive in understanding the rules exactly, and are not defined in the first few pages of the text, if at all. The terms to be defined appear here in alphabetical order.

CHAIR. The presiding officer or the position from which that person presides.

FLOOR. The position of persons other than the presiding officer (and his associates, such as the secretary and other officers) or the right to have the attention of group. Thus, when a motion is "on the floor," it is the topic to which the group should direct its attention. When a member "has the floor," he has the opportunity to exercise his speaking rights and should be given attention.

FORM. Typical wording (but not a rule), usually applied to motions or documents.

MEETING. An official gathering of members in one area to transact business for a period during which there is no interruption longer than a recess. For a complete explanation, *see* Section 42.

MEMBER. A person with the right to full participation, including the right to vote.

MOTION. A formal proposal by a member in a meeting that the assembly take certain action. The proposal is formal in that it has a wording described in this book; it is also formal in that it is not casual—that is, it is not a mere remark in a speech. The motion is a proposal in that it sets forth something the person making the motion favors. The motion must be made by a member, not a guest. The motion must occur in the context of a meeting, not before or after or otherwise apart from a meeting. The motion must refer to the assembly, but it may meet that requirement by a reference to the organization as a whole, an officer representing the assembly, a committee, or any other agent. The word *take* means only that the motion must involve a verb, such as *shall,* although the verb may be merely implied. The expression "certain action" can refer to any specified occurrence, substantive or otherwise; for instance, the "action" could be nothing more than an opinion.

PENDING. Being processed by the chair. A motion that has been stated (that is, officially announced) by the chair but not yet disposed of is said to be pending (or "on the floor"). When more than one motion is pending, the one that is directly under consideration and being given priority is said to be the immediately pending motion.

PRECEDENCE. Priority or rank, applied to motions. If motion B takes precedence over motion A, motion B is in order when motion A is pending and merits consideration at the time. Motion A thus temporarily yields to motion B. When members propose motions, they must move upward in the order of precedence; later, the same motions will be put to vote in the sequence of "last made, first voted," which will be downward in the order of precedence. Motions that have a *fixed* rank are listed in Part 1 of the "Compendium of Rules on Motions" earlier in this book; other motions vary in their rank, depending on what other parliamentary motion, if any, is being considered when they are introduced.

QUESTION. A synonym for *motion*. (When members exclaim, "Question!" they are informally calling for a vote on a motion. Concerning the handling of such, *see* Section 21.)

SESSION. One or more connected meetings transacting a single order of business. For a complete explanation, *see* Section 43.

TABLE. The desk—and, by extension, the care—of the secretary; thus, laying on the table means entrusting to the care of the secretary.

Darwin Patnode

ARTICLE I: INTRODUCTION OF BUSINESS

[Sections 1–5]

---

1. General method. All business should be brought before the assembly by a motion of a member or by the presentation of a communication to the assembly (ending in an implied motion). In many cases in the ordinary routine of business, however, it is not usual to make a motion. Instead, the chair specifies an action and announces that, if there is no objection, the action will be considered adopted. If no member says, "Objection!" or, "I object," the chair announces, "There being no objection, the action is adopted." If a member objects, a motion to take such action becomes necessary. The procedure for deciding on an action without a motion processed all the way through a vote is called general or unanimous consent.

2. Obtaining the floor. Because business requires a motion, it is usually necessary for a member to make a motion, and before a member can make a motion or address the assembly on any motion, it is necessary that he obtain the floor; that is, he must obtain the right to speak. To do so, he must be the first person to rise in his place when no one else has the floor and address the chair by title, preceded by "Mr." or "Madam," as in "Mr. Chairman" or "Madam President." (If the group prefers, it may adopt a special rule of order designating a different method of address.) The chair will then announce the member's name (the process being known as recognizing the member), thereby assigning him the right to speak.

When two or more members rise and address the chair at the same time, the chair must make a decision about which member to recognize, and he should serve the interests of the assembly by allowing the floor to alternate between the friends and the enemies of a motion, if he knows them. Furthermore, the member upon whose motion the subject under consideration was brought before the assembly (the reporting member, in the case of a committee report) is entitled to be recognized as having the floor if he has not already had it during that consideration, and a member who has not spoken on the motion is entitled to be recognized in preference to one who has.

From the decision of the chair in assigning the floor, any two members may appeal (*see* Section 14). Where there is a doubt, expressed either by the chair or by such an appeal, the chair allows the assembly to decide the question by a vote—the member getting the majority vote being entitled to the floor.

After the floor has been assigned to a member, he cannot be interrupted by calls for the question, motions to adjourn, or other devices, either by the chair or by another member, except by a point of order, another of the motions listed as being in order when another has the floor (*see* the "Compendium of Rules on Motions"), or a procedure set forth in the section on disciplinary actions. When a member needs to interrupt another member, he should rise, address the chair, and state at once the purpose for which he rises, such as "to a point of order," so that both the chair and the interrupted member understand and can act on the interruption. The interrupted member should take his seat, and the chair should proceed. Whenever any member is speaking, the chair should protect him in his right to address the assembly without interruption, except as just described.

3. Motions. Before any subject is open to debate, three steps are necessary. The first is that a motion, as defined near the end of the Preface, be made. The second is that it be seconded; that is, another member rises and—without waiting for recognition—says, "I second the motion," or just, "Second!" Such action does not mean that the seconder endorses the motion, but only that he wishes to have the motion considered. (Some motions, including points of order, do not require seconds, but most do. *See* the "Compendium of Rules on Motions.") The third step is that the motion be stated (that is, announced) by the presiding officer. When the motion is in writing, it should be handed to the chair to assist in the statement of the question, and the chair may decline to state the question on any main motion, amendment, or motion to commit, if it is not in writing.

These steps do not prevent suggestions of alterations *before* the question is stated by the chair. On the contrary, much time can be saved by such brief informal remarks, which, however, must never be allowed to run into debate and are made at the discretion of the presiding officer. The member who offers the motion, until it has been stated by the chair, can modify his motion or even withdraw it entirely; after it is stated, he can do neither without the consent of the assembly by a majority vote. When the mover modifies his motion before it has been stated by the chair, the member who seconded it can withdraw his second, but he must take the initiative to do so; the chair does not inquire.

4. Opening debate. The chair opens debate on a debatable motion by saying, after his statement of it, "Are you ready for the question?" This language is simply an invitation to debate the motion and should not be taken as implying that the chair wants to vote on the motion immediately. Debate and voting proceed as described in later sections. After a motion has been stated by the presiding officer, it is in the possession of the assembly for consideration, including the application of other motions to it. After statement, therefore, the mover cannot withdraw or modify it, except by requesting permission to withdraw or modify it or by moving an amendment to it (both processes being decided by a majority vote of the assembly, not by the member himself).

5. Dividing a motion. Although a motion may be complicated and capable of being made into several motions, no one member can insist upon its being divided; his option is to move that the motion be divided, specifying precisely how. This motion to divide the question is like an amendment. It requires a second, is not debatable, and is amendable. Any member preferring that the motion be divided differently may move to amend the division. A majority vote decides if a motion will be divided. When a motion is to be divided, each separate new motion must be a proper one for the assembly to consider, even if the other new motions are rejected. Thus, a motion to commit with instructions is indivisible, because if it is divided and the motion to commit is rejected, the motion to instruct the committee would be nonsensical, as there is no committee to instruct. Likewise, a motion to amend by striking out and inserting is indivisible, and a motion to divide a question in such a way that rewriting beyond the clerical level is required is not permitted.

Although explained here and normally offered promptly after the statement of the question, a motion to divide the question may be made at any time before voting has begun. A division of the question is an incidental motion, as discussed later.

If a motion contains two or more parts *on different subjects* and each part could stand alone, any member may *demand* that the motion be divided into its obvious parts, and the chair must comply. Such a procedure, known as division on demand, is likely to occur only when a committee makes many recommendations on different topics, as might be the case with a resolutions committee.

ARTICLE II: CLASSIFICATION OF MOTIONS

[Sections 6–9]

---

6. Main (or principal) motions. A motion that brings before the assembly, for its consideration, any particular subject independent of any other pending motion or parliamentary situation is a main motion. It can be made only when no other motion is pending, and it must be capable of standing by itself—that is, of being independent. (It may, in some cases, *refer* to past or future motions.) A main motion is almost always the first step in any parliamentary activity.

It is the lowest in rank of the ranked motions; that is, it is at the bottom of the order of precedence (*see* Part 1 of the "Compendium of Rules on Motions"). Therefore many motions may interrupt its consideration, but it interrupts the consideration of nothing. A main motion requires a second, is debatable, and is amendable. It normally takes a majority vote, except when it has the effect of changing something already adopted (such as the by-laws) or suspending a rule of order, in which case it requires a two-thirds vote, perhaps with previous notice (*see* Sections 18, 28, and 49).

7. Subsidiary motions. Subsidiary motions are motions applied to other motions for the purpose of disposing of them. There are seven such motions, and they take precedence of main motions and must be decided, if they are offered, before a final decision on the main motion. They yield to higher-ranking motions, such as privileged motions, and to incidental motions. The following are the subsidiary motions as they appear in the order of precedence:

Lay on the table
Order the previous question
Limit or extend limits of debate
Postpone definitely
Commit or refer
Amend
Postpone indefinitely

Any of these motions can be applied to the main motion, and some of them may be applied to other motions, as explained in later sections.

8. Incidental motions. Incidental motions are motions that arise out of other motions and consequently must usually be decided before the motions that gave rise to them. They are not substantively related to the other motions and may arise for a relatively minor reason, such as some detail of the method of considering another motion; thus they are aptly called incidental. They yield to privileged motions except when they arise out of privileged motions. Usually they cannot be debated or amended, and they have no fixed order of precedence; they take their rank from the motion out of which they arise. The most common incidental motions are the following:

Point of order
Appeal
Object to the consideration of a question
Divide the question

Divide the assembly
Read papers
Withdraw or modify a motion
Suspend the rules

9. Privileged motions. Privileged motions are given high rank because of their importance, taking precedence of most other motions (including all other motions in the order of precedence). They are undebatable, for otherwise their high rank would make them useful for unjustifiably consuming a large amount of time. They are only four in number, and they appear here in their order of precedence:

Adjourn
Recess
Raise a question of privilege
Call for the orders of the day

ARTICLE III: INDIVIDUAL MOTIONS

(Privileged Motions)

10. Adjourn. To adjourn is to end a meeting. This motion is usually a privileged motion but sometimes a main motion. When privileged, it takes precedence of all other ranked motions. It requires a second, is undebatable, is amendable, requires a majority vote for adoption, and cannot be reconsidered. Any amendment to a privileged motion to adjourn is undebatable. It is a main motion if it provides the final adjournment of a convention or a mass meeting. When a committee is finished with any business referred to it and is prepared to report, a committee member should make a motion "to rise," which is, in committee, the same as to adjourn.

The effect of an adjournment on unfinished business follows three rules.

When the adjournment does not close the session, the business interrupted by the adjournment is resumed immediately after the reading of the minutes at the next meeting, and the new meeting is simply a continuation of the meeting of which it is an adjournment.

When the adjournment closes a session in an assembly that meets at least quarterly, then the unfinished business is taken up at the next succeeding regular session prior to new business, and it is treated as if there had been no interruption.

When the adjournment ends a session in an assembly that does not meet at least quarterly, or when the assembly is a body elected for a definite time and this session ends the term of a portion or all of the members, the adjournment puts an end to all business unfinished at the time. The business can be introduced as new business at the next session, as if it had never been before the body.

11. Recess. To recess is to adjourn for only a short intermission (not overnight). After a recess, business is resumed at the point where it was interrupted, and the minutes are not read previously. The motion to recess is privileged *only* if made when no other motion is pending. If it is not privileged, it is treated as a main motion. If it is privileged, it is ranked just below the motion to adjourn; and it requires a second, is not debatable, is amendable, requires a majority vote for adoption, and is not reconsiderable. Any amendment to a privileged motion to recess is undebatable. Some typical wordings are "to recess until 8:00 P.M.," "to recess for twenty minutes," and "to recess until called to order by the chair." A motion to recess at a future time is always a main motion.

12. Raise a question of privilege. Questions relating to the rights and benefits of the assembly or one or more of its members are called questions of privilege, and they take precedence of all other motions of fixed rank except to recess and to adjourn. They typically involve the comfort of members; ability to hear or see speakers; conduct of officers, members, employees, and guests; or the accuracy of published reports of proceedings. (They should *not* be confused with privileged questions, which are the top four motions of fixed rank.) A motion to close the meeting to all but members (that is, to go into executive session) is a common example. If necessary, raising a question of privilege may interrupt a member's speech. In such a case, the chair may rule the question is not in order *at the time* because it is of insufficient urgency to interrupt a speech.

A member rises, addresses the chair, and then, without waiting, says, "I rise to a question of privilege." The chair directs him to state his question. The member briefly expresses his complaint and proposes, as a motion, a solution. The solution motion is the actual question of privilege, and the chair should attempt to process it by general consent (*see* Section 1). If general consent fails, the chair should ascertain if there is a second to the motion and then process it as a main motion (even if a main motion was interrupted). Thus, raising the question is a privileged process; the question itself is treated as a main motion.

It is not necessary that the assembly take final action on the question of privilege when it is raised—it may be referred to a committee, laid on the table, or have any other subsidiary motion applied to it. In such a case the subsidiary motion has no effect on the business interrupted by the question of privilege—it applies only to the motion that is the question of privilege. As soon as the interrupting question of privilege is disposed of, the assembly resumes consideration of the question that was interrupted.

13. Call for the orders of the day. A call for the orders of the day is a motion urging compliance with an agreement concerning the timing of an item of business, such as another motion. It takes precedence over all motions except those of fixed rank above it, the motion to reconsider, and the motion to suspend the rules in connection with the orders of the day. It is in order when another has the floor, does not require a second, is undebatable, is unamendable, and is a demand that must be automatically obeyed unless the assembly overturns it as described below. It is not reconsiderable.

Orders of the day are items of business scheduled *by vote* for a certain session, meeting, or time, either by themselves or with others (as in the case of an adopted agenda). Orders are of two kinds: general and special (the latter taking priority). General orders are items scheduled by a majority vote, either through postponement or through adoption of an agenda or other main motion. Special orders are scheduled by a two-thirds vote, either through a postponement or a main motion containing the words "special order" or through adoption of an agenda that sets a precise time for a specific item. Motions set as orders of the day cannot be considered before that time except by a motion to suspend the rules, which requires a two-thirds vote.

When the time arrives for taking up an order, the chair must proceed with a knowledge of whether the order is a general order or a special order. If no motion is pending, the chair should announce the order. If a motion is pending and the order is a general one, the chair should wait until the pending motion has been disposed of and then announce the order. If a motion is pending and the order is a special one, the chair should interrupt. In the event that the special order was set by an agenda, the chair should put the pending motion to a vote without further debate, although he should allow motions to lay on the table, to postpone definitely, and to refer to a committee (with no debate on such motions), as well as a motion to suspend the rules. In the event that the special order was not set by an agenda, the chair should not put the pending motion to a vote but just announce that its consideration will be resumed after disposition of the special order.

If the chair does not act in accordance with the above rules, any member may call for the orders of the day by rising, addressing the chair, and—without waiting—saying that he calls for the orders of the day or demands "the regular order." (Such a call is not permitted when a motion is pending if the order is a general one; the member must wait until the motion is no longer pending.) The chair should then announce the order and the procedure that will occur, as in the above cases, unless the member has made a mistake.

If the group does not wish to proceed to the general or special order, it may suspend the rules by a two-thirds vote and continue to process the pending business.

If the chair has any doubt about the willingness of the group to proceed to the general or special order, he may ask, "Will the assembly proceed to the orders of the day?" Permitting no debate, he then takes a vote on proceeding. If there is a two-thirds vote in the *negative,* the group does not proceed to the orders; it has, in effect, suspended the rules regarding the orders.

Motions regarding orders of the day are most likely to occur when the assembly has adopted an agenda. If such an agenda specifies a precise time for an item, that fact makes it a special order.

(Incidental Motions)

14. Point of order and appeal. A point of order (sometimes called a question of order) is an assertion that a rule is being violated and a request that the rule be enforced by the chair. It takes precedence over any pending motion out of which it arises. It is in order when another has the floor, even if it is necessary to interrupt a speaker.

It does not require a second and is not debatable or amendable. It is decided by the chair, subject to appeal, and is not reconsiderable.

To make a point of order, a member simply rises and, without waiting for recognition, says, "I rise to a point of order," or just, "Point of order!" (Any other member who is speaking should temporarily resume his seat.) The chair asks the member to state his point, and the member does so, being as specific as possible without entering into debate or asking a question. When the case is simply one of improper language used in debate, a member may say, "I call the member to order," and in such a case the chair decides whether the remarks were, in fact, out of order and proceeds as described below.

The chair then rules (that is, makes a decision) on the point of order. If the point is correct, the chair says, "The point of order is well taken" and he proceeds to correct the violation. If the point is incorrect, the chair says, "The point of order is not well taken" and briefly explains the decision. The chair may seek the opinion of advisors before ruling, and advisors should give their opinions without standing. The chair should stand when making an explanation or a ruling on a point of order or otherwise.

A point of order must be raised promptly at the time when the violation occurs, except in the case of an offense of a continuing nature, as when a motion is in violation of law or the bylaws. In such a case, the point of order can be raised at any time during the continuation of the offense, which is ongoing.

It is the duty of the presiding officer to enforce the rules of the assembly, without debate or delay. It is also the right of any member who notices a breach of a rule to insist upon its enforcement. Rising to a point of order is simply taking a step to insist that the rules be enforced.

An appeal from the decision of the chair, whether the decision is made in response to a point of order or on the chair's own initiative, is permitted except when there cannot possibly be two reasonable opinions on the matter, when the matter is merely an announcement of a vote (other motions are then available), or when another appeal is already pending.

If a member objects to the chair's decision, he says, after rising, "I appeal from the decision of the chair." If the appeal is seconded, the chair defines the issue involved, explains the reasons for his decision, and says, "Shall the decision of the chair be sustained?" (The wording is to sustain the decision of the chair, not to sustain the appeal and not to sustain the chair in general, just the decision of the chair.) An appeal is debatable unless it relates to indecorum or a violation of the rules of speaking, relates to the priority of business, or is made while the immediately pending question is undebatable. If it is debatable, no member may speak more than once in debate, but the chair may defend his ruling once again at the end of the debate. An appeal is not amendable. Either a majority vote or a tie vote sustains the chair's decision, even if the chair voted to make a tie. An appeal can be reconsidered, but such action would be very unusual.

The motion to lay on the table and other subsidiary motions may be applied to an appeal when it is not essential that the matter under appeal be resolved before consideration on any interrupted motion can be resumed.

15. Object to the consideration of a question. An objection can be made to the consideration of any main motion that begins the involvement of the assembly in a substantive matter and does not propose a parliamentary step. (Thus, an objection cannot be made to a *main* motion to approve the minutes, to amend the bylaws, to recess, and so forth.) Such an objection is a motion to block the consideration of a main motion, perhaps because the main motion would prove more embarrassing than helpful to the organization even to consider. It can be made only when the main motion is first introduced, before it has been debated or any subsidiary motion has been applied to it. It is similar to a point of order and can be made while another member has the floor. It does not require a second, is not debatable or amendable, and cannot have any subsidiary motion applied to it. The chair may state an objection to the consideration of a motion on his own initiative.

When such an objection is made (no reason should be given), the chair should immediately say, "Shall the question [or "motion"] be considered?" If decided in the *negative* by a two-thirds vote, the question cannot be considered during that session. If not decided in the negative, the discussion continues as if this motion had never been made. A negative vote (that is, one sustaining the objection) can be reconsidered; an affirmative vote cannot.

The object of this motion is not to cut off debate, for which other motions are provided, but to enable the assembly to avoid altogether any motion that it may deem irrelevant, unprofitable, or contentious. Despite the similarity of terminology, an objection to consideration should not be confused with objection to unanimous or general consent (*see* Section 1).

16. Read papers. When papers (that is, communications) or motions are put before the assembly, every member has a right to have them read once before debate and once after debate. Whenever a member asks for another reading of any such paper, evidently for information and not for delay, the chair should direct it to be read by the secretary, unless there is an objection.

A member does not, however, have a right to read a paper (including a book) *as a part of his speech,* but there is seldom an objection to a short, relevant quotation. If there is objection to reading, a member may move "that permission to read a paper in debate be granted." This motion requires no second unless moved by the person seeking to read. It is not debatable or amendable, and it requires a majority vote to grant permission. It can be reconsidered.

17. Withdraw or modify a motion. When a motion has been made but not yet been stated by the chair, whether or not it has been seconded, it can be withdrawn or modified by the mover. The member simply rises and says, for instance, "Mr. President, I withdraw the motion." If he wishes to modify the motion, he should specify the modification. Any member may suggest that the mover withdraw or modify his motion, but only the mover may do so. If a motion is modified before being stated by the chair, the seconder may withdraw his second.

After a motion has been stated by the chair, however, it is the property of the assembly, and the procedure for withdrawing or modifying it is less simple. It may be withdrawn or modified at any time before voting has begun, by the following method. The mover, with or without a suggestion from another member, rises and says, for example, "Mr. President, I ask permission to withdraw [or "modify"] the motion [specifying the method, in the case of modifying]." The chair attempts to get general or unanimous consent to withdraw or modify. If consent is given, the motion is announced as withdrawn or modified. If consent is not given, the chair assumes, in the case of modifying, a motion to amend (or any member may move an amendment); in the case of withdrawing, the chair can immediately take a vote on allowing the withdrawal, or any member can move that permission to withdraw the motion be granted. (A second is required if the mover of this motion is the mover of the original motion.) This incidental motion to give permission is undebatable and unamendable. It requires a majority vote. It may be reconsidered only in the negative.

If a motion is withdrawn, the effect is the same as if it had never been made. It does not appear in the minutes, and it can be offered again later in the meeting.

18. Suspend the rules. This motion is to render *temporarily* ineffective one or more rules of order (that is, rules in this manual or special rules of order adopted by the assembly) or standing rules. It cannot have an effect beyond adjournment. It requires a second, is not debatable or amendable, cannot have any subsidiary motion applied to it, and requires a two-thirds vote if applied to a rule of order and a majority vote if applied to a standing rule. It cannot be reconsidered. Rules contained in the bylaws cannot be suspended unless they provide for their own suspension. Thus, if the bylaws provide that an election shall be by ballot or that amendments to the bylaws shall be adopted only after previous notice, it is not permissible to suspend such a rule, even by a unanimous vote. No rule may be suspended in the face of a negative vote as large as the minority that the rule protects.

The form of this motion is "to suspend the rules [for a specified purpose]." The motion may, in effect, be combined with other motions, including main motions, as in the following: "to suspend the rules and adopt the following resolution. . . ." In such cases, the rules governing the motion to suspend the rules still apply.

A motion to suspend a certain rule for an entire session is a main motion requiring a two-thirds vote.

A motion to suspend a certain rule for a time longer than a session is a main motion to adopt a special rule of order (*see* Section 49), requiring a two-thirds vote with previous notice.

19. Other incidental motions. There are several other incidental motions discussed elsewhere in this manual. Dividing a motion, for instance, is treated in Section 5. Incidental motions related to voting are treated in Section 38. Those related to minutes are treated in Section 51. Those related to blanks and nominations are treated in Sections 26 and 27. Those related to committee reports are discussed in Sections 29 and 30. There are yet other incidental motions, and they are discussed here.

A parliamentary inquiry is an incidental motion asking the presiding officer a question on parliamentary law or the bylaws or other rules. The inquiry must be closely related to the business at hand and not hypothetical. The member with the parliamentary inquiry rises and, without obtaining the floor, says, for instance, "Mr. President, a parliamentary inquiry, please." The chair directs the member to state his inquiry, which must be stated *as a question*. The chair replies to the inquiry, but the reply is an opinion, not a ruling of the chair, and no point of order can be raised against it and no appeal can be taken from it. A member may, however, act contrary to the opinion of the chair, and the chair may then rule that act not in order (thus permitting an appeal). A parliamentary inquiry may, if necessary, interrupt a speaker. It requires no second, is undebatable, is unamendable, and is decided by the chair. It cannot be reconsidered.

There is also a motion to set the effective time of a motion. Often when an important motion is about to be adopted, some members will seek to make it effective at a later time. Motions take effect immediately upon their adoption, unless they provide otherwise or an incidental motion adopted in advance of the adoption of the main motion sets a different effective time. A motion to set the effective time can be applied to any pending main motion. It is not in order when another member has the floor, must be seconded, is debatable, is amendable, requires a majority vote, and can be reconsidered. After the adoption of the main motion, it can be reconsidered only if the main motion is reconsidered.

(Subsidiary Motions)

20. Lay on the table. The motion to lay on the table is to remove the main motion from consideration and entrust it to the care of the secretary until its consideration is resumed by the assembly at an unspecified future time. It takes precedence over all other subsidiary motions and yields to privileged and other motions. It is not in order when another member has the floor, requires a second, is undebatable, is unamendable, requires a majority vote, and cannot be reconsidered. No other subsidiary motion can be applied to it.

The form of the motion is "to lay the question on the table." The motion cannot specify a time for resumption; if it did, it would be equivalent to a motion to postpone definitely (which might be in order and perhaps even preferable).

The object of the motion is to postpone the main motion in such a way that at a future time it can be taken up when the assembly wishes rather than at a specific time set in advance. It also is sometimes used to suppress a question. When this motion is adopted, it delays consideration not only of a main motion but of any amendments and other motions that must be decided before the main motion can be decided. (If a question of privilege has interrupted the consideration of a main motion and is laid on the table, it does not take with it to the table the interrupted main motion.)

If debate has been closed, then up until the moment of taking the final vote a motion may still be laid on the table.

It is not permissible to apply a motion to lay on the table to an entire group of motions or a group of items of business, such as committee reports.

When the assembly wishes to resume consideration of a motion laid on the table, any member may, when no other member has the floor, rise, address the chair, and upon recognition, move to take a certain motion from the table. Such a motion requires a second, is undebatable and unamendable, and requires a majority vote. It cannot be reconsidered. (To take from the table is not a subsidiary or an incidental motion; it is a miscellaneous motion.) If it is adopted, the chair announces the main motion (and any other motions that were on the table with it), and their consideration is resumed. It would be in order to lay the motion on the table again after further consideration.

If a motion is laid on the table and not taken from the table, it may expire on the table. In an assembly that does not meet at least quarterly, it expires upon adjournment of the session at which it was laid on the table. In an assembly that does meet at least quarterly, it expires upon adjournment of the next regular session after that at which it was laid on the table.

21. Close, limit, or extend limits of debate. The motion to close debate has a technical name: to order the previous question. Unfortunately, this technical name can convey a wrong impression of its import; it really has nothing to do with the subject previously under consideration. It is, of course, a motion to close debate on the *pending* motion(s), with the assembly immediately proceeding to vote (unless a high-ranking motion, such as to lay on the table, intervenes). The chair should take a motion "to close debate" or "that debate cease" or "that we vote now" to be a motion to order the previous question and explain his action to members unfamiliar with parliamentary terminology. This motion takes precedence over every debatable or amendable motion to which it is applied and over the subsidiary motion to limit or extend limits of debate. It yields to the motion to lay on the table, to all privileged motions, and to all applicable incidental motions. It is not in order when another member has the floor, requires a second, is not debatable or amendable, cannot have any other subsidiary motion applied to it, and requires a two-thirds vote for adoption. It is reconsiderable but only if the vote is affirmative before it has been executed, even in part. It can be applied to any debatable or amendable motion, but it is not possible to make a motion and at the same time move to order the previous question on it, except by suspending the rules.

When a member wishes to have the previous question ordered, he obtains the floor and, upon recognition, says, "I move the previous question." If his motion is seconded, the chair immediately says, "The previous question is moved on [the motion(s) to which it applies]. Those in favor of ordering the previous question will rise," and so forth. If the motion obtains a two-thirds vote, debate is closed, and the chair proceeds to put to vote the motion(s) on which previous question was ordered. If the motion does not obtain a two-thirds vote, debate continues.

The motion for the previous question can be applied to one or more pending motions in sequence. Thus, if the pending motions are a main motion, a primary amendment, a secondary amendment, and a motion to commit, the previous question, if unqualified, applies only to the motion to commit; but it can be qualified to apply to two, three, or four of the motions, as long as it leaves no gap. (For example, it could not be applied to the motion to commit and the main motion only.) The mover who wants to apply it to more than one motion must so specify when offering his motion; in the case given, he could move the previous question on the motion to commit and the secondary amendment or on the motion to commit and both amendments or on all pending motions. The mover must so specify when offering his motion, because the motion for the previous question cannot be amended in this or any other regard.

When all required votes have been taken under an adopted order for the previous question (or after it has been voted to refer to a committee), the previous question is said to be exhausted. If a high-ranking motion interrupts the taking of vote under an adopted order for the previous question, that motion cannot be debated or amended, because the order for the previous question is presumed to apply to it. (If a question of privilege occurs during the execution of an order for the previous question, it is debatable and amendable, because the order for the previous question is presumed not to apply to it.) In the unlikely event that one of these votes is reconsidered before the previous question is exhausted, the reconsideration is undebatable.

The previous question may be ordered on a motion that is amendable but not debatable for the purpose of preventing further amendments. Thus, in the case of a privileged motion to recess, for example, the previous question may be ordered; if adopted, it would prevent the offering of any amendment to change the time involved in the recess.

To illustrate the effect of the previous question under different kinds of circumstances, take the following examples.

Suppose a question is before the assembly and an amendment to it is offered, then it is moved to postpone the question to another time. The previous question, if ordered in its unqualified form, would now stop the debate and force a vote on the pending motion—the postponement. When that vote has been taken, the effect of the previous question is exhausted. If the assembly refuses to postpone, the debate is resumed upon the pending amendment.

Suppose again that, while an amendment to the main motion is pending, a motion is made to refer the main motion to a committee, and someone moves to amend this last motion by giving the committee instructions, such as a deadline. In addition to the main question, there are motions to amend and to commit; therefore the previous question, as so specified by the mover, applies to them all. If the previous question is ordered, the chair puts to vote the amendment giving the committee instructions, then the motion to commit, then the amendment to the main motion, and finally the main motion. If, however, the motion to commit is adopted, the process ends there, and the motion for the previous question is exhausted.

Sometimes members will call, "Question!" from their seats. Such calls are *not* motions for the previous question and certainly should not be processed as motions, for doing so would merely encourage such actions. They are only informal expressions of a desire to proceed to vote. If such calls become disorderly, the chair should admonish the members, explaining that the proper procedure is to obtain recognition and *move* the previous question.

Immediately below the motion for the previous question in rank is another subsidiary motion, to limit or extend limits of debate. This motion is similar to the motion for the previous question but cannot be used to gain an immediate vote; that is, it cannot be used to limit debate to zero minutes. It may, however, serve a useful purpose. It can accomplish restrictions on debate that will eventually lead to its closing. For example, a member may move to limit debate to a total of thirty minutes, or he may move to limit debate to two additional speeches on each side (pro and con), or he may move that debate be limited to 3:00 P.M. Likewise, the motion may extend the limits on debate that this manual imposes (two speeches per person, per motion, per day, no speech in excess of ten minutes, and no second speeches while others are still seeking to give a first speech). For example, it would be in order to extend the limits of debate to permit speeches no longer than fifteen minutes or three speeches per person. It is even possible to combine the two forms of this motion: to limit speeches to one per person but extend that speech to a maximum of fifteen minutes.

A motion to limit or extend limits of debate takes precedence over all debatable motions. It yields to the motion for the previous question and the motion to lay on the table as well as all privileged motions and all applicable incidental motions. Like the motion for the previous question, it can be applied to one or more pending motions in sequence, without a gap. It is out of order when another has the floor, must be seconded, is not debatable, is amendable (but the amendment is undebatable), requires a two-thirds vote for adoption, and can be reconsidered (without debate) at any time before it is exhausted.

If debate is limited or its limits extended by this motion, a motion for the previous question may still override any such decision.

Furthermore, an adopted motion to limit debate applies not only to the motion(s) on which the limitation is ordered but also to any debatable subsidiary motions, motions to reconsider, and debatable appeals that may be made subsequently while the motion is still in force. If a motion on which debate has been limited is referred to a committee, it is not bound by those limits when reported back from the committee.

If an adopted motion to limit debate specifies a time for the close of debate, either by mentioning that time or giving a total amount of time allowed for debate, it is not in order to move to commit or postpone definitely unless the motion to limit debate is first reconsidered and then rejected, because the implication of such wordings of the motion to limit debate is that the matter will not be postponed definitely or committed before the specified time.

No motion for the previous question or to limit or extend the limits of debate remains in effect after adjournment of the session at which it was adopted.

22. Postpone definitely. This motion, also known as to postpone to a certain time or day, takes precedence of motions to commit or refer, to amend, and to postpone indefinitely. It yields to privileged or incidental motions as well as motions to lay on the table or to limit or extend the limits of debate or to order the previous question. It is not in order when another member has the floor, requires a second, is debatable (but this debate must not go into the merits of the main motion further than is necessary to enable the assembly to judge the propriety of the postponement), and is amendable (for instance, by altering the time). The motion for the previous question can be applied to it without affecting other pending motions. This motion requires a majority vote and can be reconsidered. If the motion to postpone includes the words "make a special order," it requires a two-thirds vote for adoption (*see* Section 13 for more information on special orders).

This motion may take many forms, including the following: "I move to postpone the motion to the next meeting"; "I move to postpone the motion until 8:00 P.M."; "I move to postpone the motion until 7:30 P.M. at our next meeting"; "I move to postpone the motion until the conclusion of the program"; "I move to postpone the motion until 2:00 P.M. and make it a special order."

In a group that meets at least quarterly, it is not permissible to move to postpone a motion beyond adjournment of the next regular session; in a group that meets less often than quarterly, it is not permissible to move to postpone a motion beyond adjournment of the present session. Thus, a motion cannot be postponed from one annual meeting to the next annual meeting.

Unless specified otherwise in the motion to postpone, a postponed motion is taken up by the chair as part of unfinished business.

23. Commit or refer. This motion (called recommit when the matter has been previously committed) sends a pending motion to a committee or board. It takes precedence of the motions to amend and to postpone indefinitely, and it yields to higher-ranking subsidiary motions, to privileged motions, and to all applicable incidental motions. It is not in order when another member has the floor, requires a second, is debatable, is amendable, requires a majority vote, and is reconsiderable if the committee has not begun consideration of the matter. It can be amended by changing the committee, the instructions to the committee, or other provisions. To refer a *general subject* rather than a pending motion to a committee is a main motion.

The simple form of this motion is, "to refer the motion to a committee." When different committees are proposed, either as amendments or as suggestions, they should be voted on in the following order: first, committee of the whole; second, a standing committee; third, a special committee. The number of members of the committee is often included in the motion, and sometimes even their names are specified, while in other cases the method of appointment is given. Such details should be decided, by amendment, if necessary, before adoption of the motion to commit. The instructions may include a quorum (if it is to be other than a majority) and the authorization to appoint subcommittees beyond its own membership. It is usually prudent to include in the motion some instructions and a reporting date for the committee.

If the committee is a select one and there is no provision for appointment of its members, the chair should inquire how the committee will be appointed. Sometimes the chair is given authority to appoint the members, in which case he names the members of the committee before adjournment and no vote is taken on them. In other cases the committee members are nominated, either by the chair or by members of the assembly, and then they are all appointed together by one vote (or if the number exceeds the number specified in the motion, some are elected).

Committees exist for study (perhaps with recommendations to be made) or for action (for making arrangements for an event, for instance)—or for both. If the former, the members should represent various views, so that in committee the fullest discussion may take place; if the latter, the members should all be in favor of the proposed activity.

In ordinary assemblies, by judicious appointment of committees, debates upon delicate and troublesome questions can be mostly confined to committee, which will contain representative members of all parties.

The power to appoint members of a committee includes the power to fill vacancies in that committee's membership and to remove appointees.

24. Amend. The motion to amend, that is, to change the words of a pending motion, is one of the most important in all parliamentary law, but takes precedence of nothing but the motion that it proposes to amend, and it yields to privileged, subsidiary, and incidental motions, except to postpone indefinitely. It is not in order when another member has the floor, requires a second, and is debatable (if the motion to be amended is debatable). It is amendable, except an amendment to an amendment is not amendable. Thus, amendments of the first degree and the second degree are permitted; amendments of the third degree are not. These amendments are sometimes termed primary, secondary, and tertiary, with tertiary amendments not being permitted. To amend requires a majority vote and is reconsiderable.

An amendment must be germane (that is, closely related) to the motion to be amended (not just to some pending motion). If it is not, the chair should rule it out of order, or any member may make the point of order that the amendment is not germane. From any decision of the chair on the germaneness of an amendment, a member may appeal. Such an appeal is debatable.

Certain other amendments are not in order. An amendment that would, in effect, change one parliamentary motion or form of amendment into another is not in order. Thus, it is not in order to move to amend the motion to postpone definitely by striking it out and inserting the words "to lay on the table." An amendment that would, if adopted, result in an incoherent wording is not in order. Furthermore, it is not in order to propose an amendment that would, if adopted, merely make the adoption of the amended motion equivalent to the rejection of the unamended motion. Thus, it is not in order to move to amend a motion to pay a certain bill by inserting the word *not* before the word *pay*. An amendment that merely strikes out an enacting word, such as *Resolved,* is not permitted.

The mere fact, however, that an amendment is hostile to or even directly conflicts with the spirit of the motion to be amended is insufficient to rule it out of order as long as it is germane. For instance, a motion of thanks could be amended by substituting for *thanks* the word *censure* or the word *disapproval.*

An amendment may be in any of the following four forms.

The first is to insert certain words. When the insertion occurs at the end of a passage in a motion, the term *add* is used instead of *insert.* The words inserted must be consecutive.

The second is to strike out certain words. The words struck out must be consecutive.

The third is to strike out certain words and insert others (the two parts of this amendment being indivisible). The words to be struck out, which must be consecutive, can be the same as the words to be inserted, which must also be consecutive; if they are different, as they usually are, the place of the inserted words must be the same as that of the words to be struck out, or else two separate amendments would be necessary.

The fourth is to substitute an entire motion on the same subject for the one pending. Obviously, the third and fourth forms are substantially the same, but the term *substitute* is used for the fourth form.

When any primary amendment is pending, it should be perfected by a secondary amendment previous to voting on it; once a primary amendment is adopted, it cannot be changed, except by a nonmodifying addition (unless the rules are suspended or a motion to reconsider it is adopted). The idea involved is, when the assembly has voted that certain language shall form part of a motion, it is not in order to modify that decision.

If a member, during the course of debate, offers what he calls a "friendly amendment" or an "editorial amendment," it should be handled by the chair as a motion to modify. That is, the chair should seek unanimous consent on the amendment (*see* Section 1); if that fails, the chair should use the normal amending procedure. The chair should not ask the mover of the original motion if he "accepts" the amendment.

An amendment is not necessary for clerical purposes; thus, it is not necessary to amend motions to change numbers sometimes prefixed to paragraphs, to replace pronouns with nouns, and so forth.

There is no limit to the number of times a motion may be amended, but no more than two amendments can be pending at any one time, and a later amendment may not interfere with an earlier adopted amendment, except as noted parenthetically above. In theory, then, a lengthy motion could be amended dozens of times.

An amendment is adopted by a majority vote, even if the motion to be amended requires a two-thirds vote.

An amendment to a motion previously adopted is not an amendment as discussed here, because it is not a subsidiary motion. (*See* Section 28 for such amendments.)

25. Postpone indefinitely. The motion to postpone indefinitely is to remove the main motion from the assembly's consideration for the session without a direct vote on it. This motion takes precedence of nothing except the main motion and yields to all other motions. It is not in order when another has the floor, requires a second, is debatable, is not amendable, and requires a majority vote for adoption. It is reconsiderable only if the vote was affirmative. It opens to debate the entire main motion that it proposes to postpone indefinitely. The previous question and motions to limit or extend limits of debate may be applied to it without affecting the main motion.

This motion effectively kills the main motion, and it is most likely to be used to dispose of main motions on which it is most prudent to avoid a direct vote. Sometimes it is used by opponents of a main motion to test their strength. If it is adopted, they have succeeded; if it is not adopted, they can assess their strength and their options more adeptly than otherwise.

If a main motion is referred to a committee while the motion to postpone indefinitely is pending, the latter motion is ignored from then onward.

(Miscellaneous Motions)

26. Create and fill blanks. When an amendable motion is pending and there is a portion of it that permits several alternative choices that, if processed by amendment, could consume a great deal of time, it is permissible to create a blank in that part of the motion and accept suggestions for filling the blank. Such a procedure is similar to amending. Thus, a motion containing an amount of money, a date, a place, or a name can best be handled in this manner.

A member may offer a motion containing a blank, or the chair can initiate the process of creating a blank by asking for general consent; if there is objection, the chair may proceed to put the matter to a vote. Furthermore, a member can move, by an incidental motion, that a blank be created. Such a motion is not in order when another person has the floor, must be seconded, is not debatable or amendable, requires a majority vote, and cannot be reconsidered.

When a blank has been created, the next step is to permit suggestions for filling the blank. If there was an item where the blank was created, that is the first suggestion. Any member can suggest, without a second, an item to fill the blank. Such suggestions are debatable but not amendable, and all the suggestions may be debated at one time. To close suggestions is the same as to close nominations (*see* next section). To close debate on the suggestions is the same as to order the previous question.

When the chair puts the suggestions to a vote, he should put them to a vote in the order in which they were offered, if they are names; in the order of probable acceptability (least popular first), if they are amounts; and the largest number, longest time, most-distant date, and so forth, first. Members may vote for or against each suggestion, and the first suggestion to get more affirmative votes than negative votes fills the blank. *No vote* is taken on remaining suggestions. Attention then turns to the motion, now with its blank filled.

27. Nominate and elect. Nominations are, in effect, proposals to fill the blank in the implied main motion "that _____ be elected." Sometimes the bylaws provide the method of nominating; if they do not, however, the assembly may determine the method. Motions related to nominations (except as noted below) are not in order when another person has the floor, must be seconded, are not debatable, are amendable, require a majority vote for adoption, and can be reconsidered. They are incidental motions and can provide any of various methods of nominating. A nominating committee and nominations from the floor are probably the two most frequent methods, and when the first method is used—even if the bylaws specify it—nominations from the floor must still be permitted after the report of the committee.

Because nominations themselves are similar to suggestions to fill a blank, the procedure is the same. Thus, without a second, any member can nominate someone else. The chair should repeat each nomination as he hears it. Such nominations are debatable, and all the nominations may be debated at one time. When everyone has had a reasonable opportunity to nominate—and not before—it is in order to close nominations (or to order that nominations cease). This incidental motion is not in order when another person has the floor, requires a second, is not debatable, is amendable, requires a two-thirds vote, and cannot be reconsidered. To reopen nominations is similar but requires a majority vote only, and it may be reconsidered only if the prevailing side is negative.

When debate has ended on the nominations, either by order of the previous question or otherwise, the chair proceeds to put the nominations to a vote. Unless there is a bylaw requirement describing the method of voting, the chair may proceed to take the vote as he would in the case of suggestions to fill a blank, asking members to vote affirmatively or negatively on each name, until one name obtains a majority in the affirmative, no further names then being put to a vote. In most cases, however, the assembly will, when the bylaws are silent, adopt a motion prescribing another method of voting (frequently by ballot), as set forth in the section on voting. The voting process in the present paragraph is called an election. An election is always by a majority vote, unless the bylaws or a special rule of order previously adopted states otherwise. An alternative sometimes provided is election by plurality—the largest number of votes obtained in a situation where three or more choices are possible. If an alternative is to be applied to an election of officers, it must be set forth in the bylaws.

Elections take effect immediately. If the candidate is present and does not decline (or if he is absent but has consented to his candidacy), he is elected. If the candidate is absent, has not consented to be a candidate, and does not immediately decline upon being notified, he is elected. If a person declines election, there is a failure to elect (not a vacancy), and the assembly may proceed to continue with the election; it should not follow rules concerning the filling of a vacancy.

Any eligible person may be elected, whether or not he was nominated. Membership is not a requirement for eligibility, although most societies elect people only from their own membership. When there is only one nominee and the bylaws require the election to be by ballot, without making an exception, the election must be conducted by ballot. If the bylaws are silent on the method of election or if they provide for election by ballot but make an exception for such a case, then the election can occur by another method, such as a voice vote or even general consent.

28. Reconsider and amend after adoption. These are two separate motions that can sometimes be used after adoption of another motion to gain a second consideration or to change something in the adopted motion. The first of these motions to be discussed is the motion to reconsider.

The motion to reconsider allows a group to consider again a motion on which a vote has been taken recently. It is in order at any time, even when another member has the floor or after the assembly has voted to adjourn (as long as the meeting hasn't been declared adjourned) during the same day as, or the next calendar day after, a motion has been voted upon, in the same session, but it cannot be processed while another question is before the assembly. In such a case, it can be seconded and stated by the chair and processed later, upon anyone's request. It must be made, except when the vote is by ballot, by a member who voted with the prevailing side. For instance, in case a motion fails to pass for lack of a two-thirds vote, a reconsideration must be moved by one who voted against the motion.

This motion can be *applied* to the vote on many but not all motions. For specific cases, the reader should consult the "Compendium of Rules on Motions." This motion cannot be amended; it is debatable or not, just as the question to be reconsidered is debatable or undebatable; when debatable, it opens up for discussion the entire subject to be reconsidered, and the previous question, if ordered while it is pending, affects only the motion to reconsider.

It can be laid on the table. In this case, the reconsideration, like any other question, can be taken from the table. The motion to reconsider, if laid on the table, carries with it the pending measure. If an amendment to a motion has been either adopted or rejected, and then a vote taken on the motion as amended, it is not in order to reconsider the vote on the amendment until after the vote on the original motion has been reconsidered. If the previous question has been partly executed, it cannot be reconsidered. If anything the assembly cannot reverse has been done as the result of a vote, that vote cannot be reconsidered.

The *effect of making* this motion is to suspend all action the original motion would have required until the reconsideration is completed, but if the motion to reconsider is not processed during the session, this effect terminates with the adjournment of the next regular session, except in an assembly having regular meetings less often than quarterly where its effect terminates at the adjournment of the current session. Thus, suppose the motion to reconsider a main motion is made, seconded, and stated by the chair but not immediately processed. The main motion cannot be executed until the reconsideration is complete or until an adjournment, as specified above.

While this motion is highly privileged as far as being made, reconsideration cannot be processed to interfere with the discussion of another subject before the assembly, but as soon as that subject is disposed of, anyone can call up the motion to reconsider, and the chair will then process it.

The *effect of adopting* this motion is to place before the assembly the original question in the exact condition it had before it was voted upon. Consequently, no one can debate the question that is reconsidered who has previously exhausted his right of debate on that question; the only resource is to discuss the question while the motion to reconsider is before the assembly. When a vote taken under the operation of the previous question is reconsidered, the question is then divested of the previous question and is open to debate and amendment, provided the previous question has been exhausted by votes taken on all the questions covered by it before the motion to reconsider was made.

A reconsideration requires only a majority vote, regardless of the vote necessary to adopt the motion reconsidered. A motion to reconsider cannot be reconsidered. No motion may be reconsidered more than once unless amended during the previous reconsideration.

To amend after adoption, the second motion mentioned earlier, is a kind of main motion, not a subsidiary motion to amend, despite its name. Its purpose is to change an adopted main motion. It cannot be applied to a main motion that has been executed in its entirety or to any part of the motion that has been executed. When it proposes to amend the motion by striking it out in its entirety, it is sometimes called a motion to rescind, repeal, or annul, but the rules are the same, regardless of the word used.

A motion to amend after adoption is not in order when another person has the floor, requires a second, is debatable, and is amendable. The amendments applied may be primary and secondary in nature, as explained in the section on amendments as subsidiary motions. To amend after adopton requires a two-thirds vote *or* a majority vote with previous notice *or* a majority of the total membership of the organization. Only a negative vote on a motion to amend after adoption can be reconsidered.

ARTICLE IV: COMMITTEES AND INFORMAL ACTION

[Sections 29–33]

----

29. Committees. It is usual, in deliberative assemblies, to have much work in the preparation or execution of matters done by means of committees. These may be "standing committees" (which are authorized for an indefinite time) or "select committees" (authorized only to fulfill a temporary purpose) or a "committee of the whole" (consisting of the entire assembly). Boards are equivalent to standing committees in their rules.

The first person named on a committee is chairman (in his absence the next-named member becomes chairman, and so on) and should act as such, unless the committee, by a majority of its members, elects another chairman, which it is competent to do. The secretary should furnish him or some other member of the committee with notice of the appointment of the committee, giving the names of the members, the matter referred to it, and such instructions as the assembly has decided on. The chairman shall call the committee together, and if there is a quorum (a majority of the committee), he should read or have read the entire resolution referred to it; he should then allow discussion and votes. The committee cannot vote to adopt the motion referred to it by the assembly, only to submit recommendations about it.

If the committee originates a main motion, it may recommend it to the assembly by vote. The committee votes on its entire report. If the main motion originates with the committee, all amendments are to be incorporated in it in the report, but if the main motion was referred, the committee cannot alter the text, but must submit the original motions intact, with its amendments (which *may* be in the form of a substitute written) on a separate sheet as a recommendation.

A committee is a miniature assembly of one or more persons that must meet together in order to transact business and usually one of its members should be appointed its clerk. Whatever is not agreed to by the majority of the members present and voting at a meeting (at which a quorum consisting of a majority of the members of the committee shall be present) cannot form a part of its report. The minority may be permitted to submit their views in writing also, either together or each member separately, but their report can be presented only with general consent or by an incidental motion to receive it. The motion takes a second is undebatable, is amendable, requires a majority, and is reconsiderable. The rules of the assembly, as far as possible, shall apply in committee; but a reconsideration of a vote shall be allowed, regardless of the time elapsed, only when every member who voted with the majority is present when the reconsideration is moved. A committee (except a committee of the whole) may appoint a subcommittee of its own members, unless the assembly determines otherwise. When the committee is through with the business assigned, a motion is made for the committee to "rise" (which is equivalent to the motion to adjourn). The chairman (or some member who is more familiar with the subject) will make its report to the assembly, as the committee decides. The committee ceases to exist as soon as the assembly receives the report, if it is not a standing committee.

The committee has no power to punish its members for disorderly conduct, its recourse being to report the facts to the assembly. No allusion can be made in the assembly to what has occurred in committee, except it be by a report of the committee or by general consent. It is the duty of a committee to meet on the call of any two of its members, if the chairman is absent or declines to call such a meeting. When a committee adjourns without appointing a time for the next meeting, it is called together in the same way as at its first meeting. When a committee adjourns to meet at another time, it is not necessary (though usually advisable) that absent members should be notified of the adjourned meeting.

Motions in committee meetings and motions recommended by committees do not require seconds.

30. Presentation of reports of committees. The form of a report is usually similar to the following.

A committee reports thus: "The committee on [insert name or subject of committee] respectfully reports," and so forth, letting the report follow.

"The committee" is sometimes changed to "Your committee" or "The undersigned, a committee."

When a minority report is submitted, it should be in this form (the majority reporting as above): "The undersigned, a minority of the committee on [name or subject]" and so forth. The majority report is the report of the *committee* and should never be made out as the report of only the majority. A minority report is often called minority views.

Reports *may* conclude with, "All of which is respectfully submitted," though these words are often omitted. They are sometimes signed only by the chairman of the committee, but if the matter is of much importance, it is better that the report be signed by every member who concurs. The report is not usually dated or addressed but is headed as, for example, "Report of the Finance Committee of the Y.P.A., on Renting a Hall." The report of a committee should usually end with formal resolutions or other motions covering all the recommendations, so the adoption of the motions will carry out its recommendations.

When the report is to be made, the member appointed to make the report informs the assembly that the committee to which was referred such a subject or paper has directed him to make a report thereon, or report it with or without amendment, as the case may be. It is not necessary to move it be "received" now or at any other time. He then reads the report. A very common error is, after a report has been read, to move that it be received, whereas the fact that it has been read shows it has been already received by the assembly. Another mistake, less commonly made, is to vote that the report be "accepted" (which is an unclear term) when the intention is only to have the report up for consideration and afterwards move its adoption. Still another error is to move that "The report be adopted and the committee be discharged" when the committee has reported in full and the report has been received. The committee has already ceased to exist. If the committee, however, has made but a partial report or an interim report, then it is in order to move that the committee be discharged from the further consideration of the subject, as would also be the case if the committee did not report on time. Such a motion is not in order when another person is on the floor, requires a second, is debatable, is amendable, and requires a majority vote. A negative vote on it is reconsiderable. The chairman of the committee delivers the report to the clerk. If the report consists of a paper with amendments, the chairman of the committee reads the amendments, explaining them and the reasons of the committee for the amendments, till he has gone through the whole report. If the report is very long, it is not usually read until the assembly has copies of it.

When the report has been presented, the committee is thereby dissolved and can act no more unless it is revived by a vote to recommit. If the report is recommitted, all parts of the report not agreed to by the assembly are ignored by the committee as if the report had never been made.

If any member or members wish to submit a minority report, it is customary to receive it by an incidental motion immediately after receiving the report of the committee. A minority report may end with motions, just as committee reports often do.

31. Adoption of reports of committees. When the assembly has considered a report, a motion *may* be made to adopt the report. That motion, if carried, makes the doings of the committee the acts of the assembly, the same as if done by the assembly without the intervention of a committee. In most cases, it is best to have no motion, and the chair will proceed with further business. (When a report contains no recommendations, it is not necessary to adopt the report; most groups prefer not to do so unless they wish to endorse the entire report strongly.) If the report contains merely a statement of opinion or facts, the form of the motion is to "adopt the report." If it concludes with recommended motions, the motion would be more appropriately worded as "to adopt the recommendations" or "to adopt the report and the recommendations." All these motions are main motions.

After any of the above motions is made, the motion is open to amendment, and the matter stands before the assembly exactly the same as if there had been no committee and the subject had been introduced by the motion of the member who made the report.

32. Committee of the whole. When an assembly has to consider a subject that it does not wish to refer to a committee, but the subject is not well digested and put into proper form for its definite action, or when, for any other reason, it is desirable for the assembly to consider a subject with all the freedom of a committee, the assembly may refer the topic or the main motion to a committee of the whole. If a main motion is pending, someone offers a motion to commit. If no main motion is pending, the motion to commit the subject becomes a main motion. In either case, it is seldom used and may confuse many members. If adopted, the chairman immediately calls another member to the chair and takes his place as a member of the committee. The committee is under the rules of the assembly, except as stated hereafter in this section.

The only motions in order are to amend and adopt and that the committee "rise," as it cannot adjourn. The only way to close or limit debate in committee of the whole is for the assembly to do so in advance by motion. If no limit is prescribed, any member may speak as often as he can get the floor and as long each time as is allowed in debate in the assembly, provided no one wishes the floor who has not spoken on that particular question. Debate having been closed at a particular time by order of the assembly, it is not competent for the committee, even by unanimous consent, to extend the time. The committee cannot refer the subject to another committee. Like other committees, it cannot alter the text of any motion referred to it; but if the motion originated in the committee, then all the amendments are incorporated in it.

When it is through with the consideration of the subject referred to it or if it wishes to adjourn or to have the assembly limit debate, a motion is made that "the committee rise." This motion "to rise" is equivalent to the motion to adjourn in the assembly. As soon as this motion is adopted, the presiding officer takes the chair, and the chairman of the committee, having resumed his place in the assembly, rises and informs him that "the committee has gone through the business referred to it and is ready [or "is not yet ready"] to report."

The clerk does not record the proceedings of the committee in the minutes but should keep a memorandum of the proceedings for the use of the committee. In large assemblies the clerk vacates his chair, which is occupied by the chairman of the committee, and the assistant clerk acts as clerk of the committee. If the committee becomes disorderly and the chairman is unable to preserve order, the presiding officer of the assembly can take the chair and declare the committee dissolved. The quorum of the committee of the whole is the same as that of the assembly. If the committee finds itself without a quorum, it can only rise and report the fact to the assembly.

33. Informal consideration. It has become customary in some assemblies, instead of going into committee of the whole, to consider the question "informally" and afterwards act "formally." In a small assembly there is no objection to this. While acting informally upon any resolutions, the assembly can only amend and adopt them, and without further motion the chairman announces that "the assembly, acting informally, has had such subject under consideration and has made certain amendments, which will be reported." The subject comes before the assembly then as if reported by a committee. While acting informally, the chairman retains his seat, as it is not necessary to move that the committee rise; but at any time the adoption of such motions as to adjourn, the previous question, to commit, or any motion except to amend or adopt puts an end to the informal consideration.

While a group is acting informally, every member can speak as many times as he pleases and as long each time as permitted in the assembly, and the informal action may be rejected or altered by the assembly. While the clerk should keep a memorandum of the informal proceedings, it should not be entered in the minutes, being only for temporary use. The chairman's report to the assembly of the informal action should be entered in the minutes, as it belongs to the assembly's proceedings. Informal consideration may confuse many members and should probably be avoided.

ARTICLE V: DEBATE AND DECORUM

[Sections 34-37]

---

34. Debate. Debate is any spoken comment on the merits of a pending motion, whether or not a clear preference for or against the motion is expressed. When a motion is made and, if necessary, seconded, it must be stated by the chair before any debate, including that of the mover, is permitted. When any member wishes to speak in debate, he must wait until no other member is speaking, then rise (not raise his hand), and address the chair. He should use the title established for the presiding officer, preceded by "Mr." or "Madam," as in "Mr. President," "Madam Chairman," etc. An organization may adopt a special rule of order providing a different style of address.

If a member rising is not known to the chair, the member may have to add his name.

The chair assigns the floor to the person, that is, grants recognition or recognizes him by announcing his name. The member who moved the adoption of the motion is first entitled to the floor, even though another member has risen first and addressed the chair. In the case of a report of a committee, preference is given to the member who presents the report. This member is *not* entitled to end the debate, however.

No member shall speak to the same motion more than twice in one day, no longer than ten minutes at one time, without permission of the assembly, and the question extending the debate for that person shall be decided by a two-thirds vote with no debate. If greater freedom is desired, the proper course is to refer the subject to the committee of the whole or to consider it informally. No member can speak the second time to a motion until every member choosing to speak has spoken. But if an amendment or any other motion is offered, that presents a new question before the assembly and presents a new right to debate. Merely asking a question or making a suggestion is not considered debating. The maker of a motion, though he can vote against it, cannot speak against his own motion. A member cannot transfer to another the right to debate.

35. Debatable and undebatable motions. Some motions are debatable and some are not. Perhaps a useful basis of distinguishing the two is that motions are debatable unless the occurrence of debate would defeat their purpose or needlessly delay action. Thus, to limit debate is not debatable, because allowing debate would frustrate its obvious purpose. Likewise, allowing debate on a motion to adjourn or a motion to recess would constitute a partial defeat for the motion, because the goal of said motion is to end or suspend the meeting promptly, not after debate. Even so, sometimes motions to adjourn or recess *are* debatable, so a knowledge of the specific rules is required; reliance on general principles or observed patterns is not enough.

Furthermore, a small number of motions opens to debate other motions. For example, the motion to postpone indefinitely opens to debate the main motion: that is, debate on the indefinite postponement may enter into the merits of the main motion.

Consulting the "Compendium of Rules on Motions" will provide a quick reference, but the prudent reader will also study the text concerning the motion.

The distinction between debate and making suggestions or asking a question should always be kept in view, and when the latter will assist the assembly in determining the question, it is allowed, to a limited extent, even though the question before the assembly is undebatable. Such matters are at the discretion of the chair.

36. Decorum in debate. In debate a member must confine himself to the question immediately before the assembly and avoid personalities. He cannot reflect upon any past act of the assembly, unless he intends to conclude his remarks with a motion to amend or reconsider such action, or else while debating such motion. In referring to another member, he should, as much as possible, avoid using his name, rather referring to him as "The member who spoke last" or in some other way describing him. The officers of the assembly should always be referred to by their official titles. It is not allowable to arraign the motives of a member, but the nature or consequences of a measure may be condemned in strong terms. It is not the man, but the measure, that is the subject of debate. If at any time the chair rises to state a point of order or otherwise speak within his privileges, the member speaking must take his seat until the chair has been heard. When called to order, a member must sit down until the question of order is decided. If his remarks are decided to be improper, he cannot proceed in the same manner.

Disorderly words should be taken down by the member who objects to them or by the clerk and then read to the member. If a member cannot justify the words used and will not suitably apologize for using them, it is the duty of the assembly to act in the case. If the disorderly words are of a personal nature, before the assembly proceeds to deliberate upon the case, both parties to the personality should retire, it being a general rule that no member should be present in the assembly when any matter relating to himself is under debate. It is not, however, necessary for the member objecting to the words to retire, unless he is personally involved in the case. If any business has taken place since the member spoke, it is too late to take notice of any disorderly words he used.

During debate or while the chair is speaking or the assembly is engaged in voting, no member is permitted to disturb the assembly by whispering, by walking across the floor, or by any other activity.

37. Ending debate. Debate of a question is not ended by the chair's rising to put the question to vote until both the affirmative and the negative are put; a member can claim the floor and thus reopen debate. Debate can be ended by the motion to order the previous question. If a member offers a motion "to close debate" or "that debate cease" or "that debate be limited to zero minutes," the chair should take it as a motion to order the previous question. If the terminology of the motion for the previous question is unclear to the members, the chair should explain its effect.

Certain motions have the effect of ending or suspending debate, but that is not necessarily their primary purpose. For instance, if the motion to lay on the table is adopted, it suspends debate on the motion laid on the table. Likewise, the adoption of an objection to the consideration of a question terminates debate on the motion.

Furthermore, the assembly may adopt motions that provide for a closing of a debate at a future time. Such motions should be taken by the chair as motions to limit debate.

A motion to permit debate on an undebatable motion is

actually a motion to suspend the rules and should be treated as such.

ARTICLE VI: VOTING

[Sections 38–39]

---

38. Voting methods. Whenever the nature of a motion permits no modification or debate, the chair immediately puts it to a vote. If the motion is debatable or amendable, when the chair thinks the process has been brought to a close, he should inquire if the assembly is ready for the question, and if no one rises he puts the question to vote. If debate is ended by a motion, he puts the question to a vote. Votes are taken by voice, by rising, by ballot, by roll call, or by any other method authorized by the assembly.

There are various forms for putting the question to a vote. The following form is the basic one when the motion requires a majority vote: "The question is on the motion to [here repeat or clearly identify the motion]. As many as are in favor of the motion, say 'aye.' Those opposed, say 'no.' The ayes have it and the motion is adopted." When the prevailing side is negative, the wording ends, "The noes have it, and the motion is lost."

When the motion requires a two-thirds vote, the following is the basic form: "The question is on the motion to [here repeat or clearly identify the motion]. Those in favor of the motion will rise [or "please stand"]. Be seated. Those opposed will rise [or "please stand"]. Be seated. There are two-thirds in the affirmative, and the motion is adopted." If there are not two-thirds in the affirmative, the wording ends, "There are less than two-thirds in the affirmative, and the motion is lost."

If a division is demanded or a count is ordered, the form is that of the two-thirds vote (above), but it ends, "The affirmative has it, and the motion is adopted," or "The negative has it and the motion is lost." If a count was taken either on the chair's initiative because the vote appeared close or because of a motion requiring a count, the numbers should be given before the above wording regarding which side has it.

When a vote is to be counted, the chair may do so or appoint tellers to make the count and report to him. When tellers are appointed, they should be selected from both sides of the question.

If the chair has doubt in deciding a voice vote, he may say, "The ayes [or "noes"] seem to have it" and then pause; if no one demands a division, he may proceed to say, "The ayes [or "noes"] have it," as given above. He may also retake the vote and count it.

In all these forms, *carried* may be used instead of *adopted,* and *rejected* may be used instead of *lost. Passed* should be avoided.

A member has the right to change his vote (when not made by ballot) before the decision of the question has been finally and conclusively pronounced by the chair, but not afterwards.

Until the negative is put, it is in order for any member, unless debate was ended by motion, in the same manner as if the voting had not been commenced, to rise, speak, make motions for amendment or otherwise, and thus renew the debate whether the member was in the assembly room or not when the question was put and the vote partly taken. After the chair has announced the vote, if it is found a member had risen and addressed the chair before the negative had been put, he is entitled to be heard on the question, the same as though the vote had not been taken. In such cases the question is in the same condition as if it had never been put.

No one can vote on a question affecting himself; but if more than one name is included in a motion (though a sense of delicacy would prevent this right from being exercised, except when it would change the vote) all are entitled to vote. If this were not so, a minority could control an assembly by including the names of a sufficient number in a motion, say for preferring charges against them, and suspend them or even expel them from the assembly. But after a member has been notified of charges and the assembly has ordered him to appear for trial, he is theoretically in arrest and is deprived of all rights of membership until his case is disposed of.

The chair, if not a member of the assembly, can never vote. If the chair is a member, he can vote when the vote is by ballot or when his vote, cast as he intends to cast it, would change the outcome. Section 50 gives details. When there is a tie vote, the motion is rejected, unless the chair gives his vote for the affirmative, which in such a case he can do. Where his vote will *make* a tie, he can cast it and thus defeat the measure. But in the case of an appeal (*see* Section 14), though the question is, "Shall the decision of the chair stand as the judgment of the assembly?" a tie vote sustains the chair, upon the principle that the decision of the chair can be reversed only by a majority. If the chair has already voted, as in the case of a ballot vote, he cannot do so again.

Another form of voting is by *ballot*. This method is used only when required by the constitution or bylaws of the assembly or when the assembly has ordered the vote to be taken by ballot. The chair, in such cases, appoints at least two tellers to assist in voting. A typical procedure is to distribute slips of paper, upon which each member, including the chair, writes his vote. (Should the chair neglect to vote before the ballots are counted, he cannot then vote without the permission of the assembly.) The votes are then collected, counted by the tellers, and the result reported to the chair, who announces it to the assembly. The chair announces the result of the vote, in case of an election to office, in a manner similar to the following: "The whole number of votes cast is _____; the number necessary for an election is _____; Mr. A received _____; Mr. B, _____; Mr. C, _____. Mr. B, having received the required number, is elected." Where there is only one candidate for an office and the bylaws require the vote to be by ballot, it is still necessary to ballot in the usual way. When a motion is made to make a ballot vote unanimous, it requires a unanimous ballot vote, and thus it may be withdrawn upon announcement of that fact. In counting the ballots, all blanks are ignored. Any method of voting that ensures secrecy constitutes a vote by ballot, even if no slips of paper are used.

The assembly can, by a majority vote, order the vote on any question be taken by roll call *(yeas and nays)*. The form of putting a question upon which the vote has been ordered to be taken by yeas and nays is similar to the following: "As many as are in favor of the adoption of this motion will, when their names are called, answer *yes;* those opposed will answer *no.*" The chair will then direct the clerk to call the roll. In this method of voting, the chair states both sides of the question at once; the clerk calls the roll; each member, as his name is called, *rises* and answers, and the clerk notes his answer. Upon the completion of the roll, the clerk reads aloud the names of those who answered in the affirmative and then those in the negative, so that mistakes may be corrected; he then gives the number voting on each side to the chair, who may vote to make or break a tie (as noted above) and announces the result. An entry must be made in the minutes of the names of all voting in the affirmative and also of those in the negative.

Taking a vote by yeas and nays, which has the effect of placing on the record how each member votes, consumes a great deal of time, and is rarely useful in ordinary societies. While it can never be used to hinder business, as long as the above rules are observed, it should not be used at all in a mass meeting or in any other assembly whose members are not responsible to a constituency.

The yeas and nays cannot be ordered in committee of the whole.

In general, the assembly can decide matters relevant to voting by an incidental motion. Such a motion is not in order when another has the floor, requires a second, is undebatable, is amendable, requires a majority vote, and is reconsiderable. A motion to order an exact count (a rising vote with more accuracy than the mere view of a division) is one such incidental motion.

A show of hands can be used in a very small assembly as an alternative to a rising vote, if no one objects.

No member is allowed to explain his vote during the voting process; such an explanation is debate and should have been offered during the course of debate.

A member must be present to vote, but he need not have been present during the debate. Furthermore, he can vote on a division or second round of voting, even if he was not present during the voice vote or first round.

If it is desired to permit absent members to vote, the bylaws must so provide. When bylaws so permit, it is usually by mail vote or by proxy vote. Both of these methods pose problems, and bylaw provisions authorizing them must be very thorough.

39. Calculating votes. All votes are calculated on the basis of present voting members. With the right to vote goes the right to abstain from voting, but the chair should never call for abstentions, nor do members have a *right* to announce that they abstained. Abstentions have no effect on calculation of votes. (When a ballot is marked "abstain," it is considered a blank.) Illegal votes are those given unclearly or for an ineligible option (such as a person not eligible for office in an election by ballot).

Unless stated otherwise, a majority is more than half of the votes cast by legal voters. Note that illegal votes *are* part of the calculation, *if* they are cast by legal voters. Note also that a majority is not necessarily *one* more than half or fifty-one percent. Thus, a majority of twenty present voting members is eleven; a majority of twenty-one is eleven; a majority of twenty-two is twelve. If there are twenty members present, but only seven vote, a majority is four.

In the case of a two-thirds vote, there must be at least two-thirds of the present voting members in the affirmative for adoption. Thus, if there are twenty present voting members, fourteen would constitute two-thirds. If there are twenty-one, fourteen would constitute two-thirds. If there are twenty-two, fifteen would constitute two-thirds.

Just as in the case of a majority there must be more in the affirmative than in the negative, so in the case of a two-thirds vote there must be at least twice as many in the affirmative as in the negative.

A unanimous vote is a vote in which no present voting

member votes contrary to the others, even if only a few of the others vote.

A plurality is the largest number of votes obtained in a situation where three or more choices are possible, such as some elections.

When tellers assist in the taking of a vote, they should report the results to the chair in such a way that all present can hear, but they should not indicate which side prevailed; they merely report numerical results, and the chair subsequently declares which side prevailed.

A majority is always competent to adopt a motion, unless the rules of order or the bylaws provide otherwise. When there is a requirement of a two-thirds vote, it is usually because the motion interferes with some basic right, such as the right to speak, or has the effect of changing something already decided.

ARTICLE VII: ORDER OF BUSINESS AND AGENDA

[Sections 40–41]

---

40. Order of business. The order of business is the general sequence of events in meetings. Each organization may adopt its own, and doing so is equivalent to adopting a special rule of order. When no order of business has been adopted, the following is the order by rule, but this rule should not be taken to interfere with the adoption by majority vote of an agenda (*see* Section 41), and it may be suspended by a motion to suspend the rules.

Reading and approval of minutes
Reports of officers, boards, and standing committees
Reports of special committees
Special orders
Unfinished business and general orders
New business

A meeting begins with a call to order. The presiding officer takes the chair, signals for attention (perhaps by rapping a gavel), and announces, "The meeting will come to order," or "The meeting will be in order."

He then calls upon the secretary to read the minutes of the previous meeting. After the reading, the chair asks, "Are there any corrections to the minutes?" If there are no corrections, the chair should announce, "There being no corrections, the minutes are approved as read." If there are corrections, the chair should attempt to process them by general consent; if that fails, they should be treated as amendments to the implied main motion of approving the minutes. When the amendments (corrections) have been decided, the chair announces, "If there are no further corrections, the minutes are approved as corrected," or he may take a vote on "approving the minutes as amended." If a member moves that the minutes be approved (or "approved as submitted" or any similar wording), the chair should process the motion as he would any other main motion, first attempting general consent (*see* Section 1). The section on the secretary and the minutes (*see* Section 51) sets forth some options at this stage.

Next, the chair announces, in turn, the reports of officers, boards, standing committees, and special committees. Officers present their reports (if they have reports) in the order in which the offices are listed in the bylaws. The president does not vacate the chair to present his report. Board reports, usually occurring only at annual meetings, may be presented by the chairman of the board or the secretary of the board. Committee reports are normally presented in the order in which the committees are listed in the bylaws (or in the case of special committees, the order in which the committees were created) by the chairman of the committee but may be presented by any designated member of the committee. A motion arising out of the report of any of the above should be processed immediately, though the assembly may vote to defer action on it. A motion recommended in an officer's report should be moved by another member, but a motion recommended in a committee's report should be moved by the person presenting the report. The chair should not call on officers, boards, or committees to report unless he knows that they have a report to present.

Special orders are defined in Section 13. They are announced by the chair.

Unfinished business involves three possible items. First is any motion actually pending when the previous meeting adjourned. Second are any motions that were unfinished business at the previous meeting but not reached before adjournment. Third are any motions set as general orders (by postponement, by an adopted agenda, or otherwise) for the previous meeting but not reached before adjournment. The chair should announce any items of unfinished business or general orders of which he is aware; he should not inquire, "Is there any unfinished business?" Likewise, he should not accede to members' claims that certain items of new business are actually items of unfinished business because their general topic was previously discussed at some time in the history of the organization.

General orders are defined in Section 13. They are announced by the chair.

For new business, the chair should inquire, "Is there any new business?" This portion of the meeting allows members to present new items of business, make announcements, and hear a program, if there is one.

A motion to take from the table a motion previously laid on the table is in order as unfinished business, as new business, or in any other part of the order of business when the motion on the table would have been in order.

When new business is complete, the meeting adjourns, either by general consent or upon motion adopted by a majority vote. Adjournment is commonly signaled by a tap of the gavel.

41. Agenda. The agenda is a detailed list of specific items arranged in an order of business. The agenda may or may not be adopted by an assembly at the beginning of a meeting. When nonbusiness matters, such as guest speakers, meals, or an educational program, are included in the agenda, it is often called a program. Having a printed copy of the tentative agenda in the hands of each member is a popular procedure. The adoption of an agenda is a kind of main motion: it is not in order when another has the floor, requires a second, is debatable, is amendable, requires a majority vote, and is reconsiderable only in the negative. After an agenda has been adopted, it may be suspended by a motion comparable to a motion to suspend the rules, and it may be amended by the motion to amend after adoption.

Frequently an agenda includes times, and such an agenda is permissible and may be adopted by a majority vote.

The following is a sample agenda without times. The reader will note that it contains more specifics than the order of business.

SAMPLE AGENDA

Call to order
Opening ceremonies
Reading and approval of the minutes
Reports of officers
    Report of the president
    Report of the treasurer
Reports of boards and committees
    Report of the standing committee on bylaws
    Report of the standing committee on finance
    Report of special committee on awards
Unfinished business and general orders
    Postponed motion on parking lot
New business
    New motion on city-council elections
    New motion on computer purchases

Other new motions
Program
Announcements
Adjournment

ARTICLE VIII: MEETING, SESSION, NOTICE, AND QUORUM

[Sections 42–45]

———————

42. Meeting. A meeting is an official gathering of members in one area to transact business for a period with no interruption longer than a recess. The gathering is official, not unauthorized. It involves members, though guests may be present. It is in one area, not over the telephone, by computers, through the mail, or otherwise in two or more locations. Its purpose is to transact business, although a program, social event, or other activity may be part of the meeting. The period of time can vary from a few seconds upward, but most meetings last an hour or more. It can have no interruption more than a few minutes or a few hours.

A recess does not terminate a meeting; it merely interrupts it for a few minutes or a few hours.

An adjournment terminates a meeting but not necessarily a session. (*See* the next section.)

The normal periodic meeting of an organization, typically held at regular intervals, is called a regular (or stated) meeting; the opposite—a meeting that is not a regular one—is called a special (or called) meeting, and it is convened only to consider one or more items of business specified in the notice of the meeting. It usually involves an emergency or a matter of such complexity that an entire meeting is needed to consider it fully. The bylaws should make provision for both regular and special meetings, including the schedule, the person(s) authorized to call them, and the number of days' notice required (*see*

Section 44). Both regular and special meetings might more precisely be called regular and special sessions.

An annual meeting is a once-a-year regular meeting designated by the bylaws for reports from all officers, boards, and standing committees, for elections, and for other matters. A few organizations hold "annual" meetings only once every two or more years, but the concept is the same. Business required by the bylaws to be transacted at the annual meeting may legitimately occur at an adjourned meeting of the annual meeting. Again, an annual meeting might more precisely be called an annual session.

43. Session. A session is one or more connected meetings transacting a single order of business. Thus, a convention of three days would consist of three meetings but only one session. Likewise, a local club, meeting monthly, might find at one meeting that it cannot transact all of its business; in such a case, it could provide for a second meeting, called an adjourned meeting, on another day, perhaps a week later, to complete its business, thus having two meetings in one session. Most local organizations transact all their business in one meeting and for them a meeting is a session.

A recess does not end a session; an adjournment may or may not end a session. If the adjournment is simply the end of a meeting and another meeting has been scheduled to continue to process the same order of business, then the adjournment does not end the session. The second meeting is called an "adjourned meeting," because it is a meeting more or less initiated by the adjournment of the first meeting. On the other hand, if the adjournment ends the meeting and no other meeting has been scheduled to continue to process the same order of business, then the adjournment ends the meeting and the session as well.

The term "adjournment *sine die*" ("adjournment without day") is optionally used to refer to the end of a session with a membership that will (unless under an emergency provision in the bylaws) never meet again, as in the case of a series of mass meetings or a convention for which the delegates are chosen for a single session. It is a ceremonial expression and does not have any impact on the motion itself, but an adjournment *sine die* is a main motion, as explained in Section 10.

Although an early meeting in a session may, to some extent, restrict a later meeting in the same session (perhaps by adopting an agenda or some other motion), no one session can interfere with the rights of a future session, except as provided in the bylaws or rules of order. The bylaws and rules of order are not subject to sudden changes (unless provided, otherwise they require previous notice of amendment) and thus may be considered as expressing the deliberate views of the whole organization rather than the opinions or wishes of any particular meeting; thus, they may be more restrictive than other motions. Of course, a session can adopt a motion of a permanent or long-term nature, and that motion stays in force until rescinded or suspended, but such a motion does not interfere with the rights of subsequent sessions, because it can be suspended at any time by a majority vote.

As a consequence of this rule, it is not in order for an assembly to postpone a motion beyond the adjournment of the next session in an attempt to prevent the next session from considering the motion. This rule does not, however, prevent instructing a committee to report at any future session.

An *executive session* is simply any meeting or part of a meeting where the proceedings are to be secret; thus, attendance of persons other than members may be severely limited. The term no longer applies solely to business unique to responsibilities of the chief executive officer. A motion to go into executive session is a question of privilege.

44. Notice. The term *notice* means either of two things in parliamentary law.

The first is notice of a meeting, which is a written announcement giving the date, time, and place of the start of a session, given to all members a reasonable time in advance. The bylaws should specify the number of days required. Notice given orally, either in person or otherwise, not being "written," does not suffice. The notice is given by the secretary. If the notice is mailed, the requirement of a certain number of days may be met by a postmark, not by the date of receipt by a member. Sometimes bylaws provide that no notice need be given of regular meetings, because such meetings are often scheduled by the bylaws themselves. Notice of a special meeting must include the items of business to be considered at the meeting, and no other items may be considered. Notice of an annual meeting should specify it involves the reception of annual reports, the election of officers, and any other business in order. If a vacancy is to be filled at any meeting, the notice should so state, as it should when the group will elect a chairman *pro tem* to serve for more than a single session. A notice of a meeting is a very important document, and no meeting is valid without a notice, unless the bylaws provide otherwise. The notice of a meeting is also known as the call of a meeting.

The second kind of notice, also known as previous notice, is an announcement of certain motions. Such notice is a written announcement given to all members a reasonable time in advance in or with the meeting notice *or* an oral announcement (if the group meets at least quarterly) made by any member at the immediately preceding meeting. The announcement must give the purport of the motion in accurate and complete terms, but it does not have to give the precise text. The oral announcement is repeated by the chair and recorded in the minutes. The written announcement is given by the secretary, upon request of a member, the same number of days in advance as would be the case for the notice of a meeting. The organization may provide by rule that the notice include the precise text, but it is seldom wise to do so. The notice of a motion limits the extent to which it can be amended; if it is amended beyond the scope of the notice, then the notice becomes invalid. The only motions *requiring* previous notice are motions to amend the bylaws or the rules of order (that is, to adopt special rules of order); other motions to amend after adoption optionally have previous notice.

45. Quorum. A quorum is the minimum number of members who must be present at a meeting for the transaction of business. Unless there is a rule to the contrary, a quorum is a majority of the members. It is usual, however, to adopt a much smaller number, the quorum often being less than one-twentieth of the members. An organization's quorum for meetings must be set in its bylaws, preferably as a fraction or a percentage rather than an absolute number.

While a quorum is competent to transact business, it is usually not prudent to transact important business unless there is a good attendance at the meeting.

The presiding officer should not take the chair until a quorum is present, unless there is no hope that a quorum will appear. When a quorum is present, the chair does not need to announce that fact unless asked. If a quorum is not present after waiting a reasonable period of time, the presiding officer should take the chair, call the meeting to order, announce the absence of a quorum, and entertain a motion to adjourn, to fix the time to which to adjourn, to recess, or to take measures to obtain a quorum. The same procedure is required if the chair notices the absence of a quorum during a meeting, either upon the chair's initiative or upon that of a member. If no member makes a point of no quorum (a point of order that no quorum is present), the chair, noticing that a quorum is no longer present, may allow debate to continue, but he should not allow any vote to be taken, except as specified above.

In committee of the whole, the quorum is the same as in the assembly; in any other committee or in a board, the quorum is a majority, unless the assembly specifies otherwise.

The rule regarding a quorum cannot be suspended, even by a unanimous vote, and it is both wrong and dangerous to transact business in the absence of a quorum.

There is no requirement, however, that a quorum vote on any given motion; it is entirely possible that members will abstain, and the rule of the quorum is merely that the members be present, not that they vote.

ARTICLE IX: ASSEMBLIES AND BYLAWS

[Sections 46–49]

---

46. Occasional or mass meetings.

(a) Organization. Some meetings are not meetings of organized societies but only occasional or one-time meetings, and their special procedures are the following.

To open the meeting, some member of the assembly steps forward and says, "The meeting will please come to order. I move that Mr. A act as chairman of this meeting." Someone else says, "I second the motion." The first member then puts the question to vote, by saying, "It is moved and seconded that Mr. A act as chairman of this meeting; those in favor of the motion will say aye." When the affirmative vote is taken, he says, "Those opposed will say no." If the majority vote is in the affirmative, he says, "The motion is carried; Mr. A will take the chair." If the motion is lost, he announces that fact, calls for the nomination of someone else for chairman, and proceeds with the new nomination as in the first case. In large assemblies, the member who nominates, with one other member, frequently conducts the presiding officer to the chair, and the chairman makes a short speech, thanking the assembly for the honor conferred on him.

When Mr. A takes the chair, he says, "The first business in order is the election of a secretary." Someone then makes a motion as just described, or he says, "I nominate Mr. B"; then the chairman puts the question as before. Sometimes several names are called out, and the chair, as he hears them says, "Mr. B is nominated; Mr. C is nominated," etc.; he eventually takes a vote on the first one he heard, putting the question thus: "As many as are in favor of Mr. B's acting as secretary of this meeting will say aye; those opposed will say no." If the motion is lost the question is put on Mr. C, and so on, till someone is elected. The secretary should take his seat near the chairman and keep a record of the proceedings.

(b) *Adoption of resolutions.* These two officers are all that are usually necessary for a meeting; so when the secretary is elected, the chairman asks, "What is the further pleasure of the meeting?" Because the meeting is merely a public assembly called together to consider some special subject, it is customary at this stage of the proceedings for someone to offer a series of resolutions previously prepared or else to move the appointment of a committee to prepare resolutions upon the subject. In the first case he rises and says, "Mr. Chairman." The chair responds, "Mr. C." Mr. C, having thus obtained the floor then says, "I move the adoption of the following resolutions," which he then reads and hands to the chairman; someone else says, "I second the motion." The chairman sometimes directs the secretary to read the resolutions again after which he says, "The question is on the adoption of the resolutions just read"; and if no one rises immediately, he adds, "Are you ready for the question?" If no one then rises, he says, "As many as are in favor of the adoption of the resolutions just read will say aye." After the ayes have voted, he says, "As many as are opposed will say no." He announces the result of the vote as follows: "The motion is carried—the resolutions are adopted," or, "The ayes have it—the resolutions are adopted."

(c) *Committee to draft resolutions.* If it is preferred to appoint a committee to draft resolutions, a member, after he has addressed the chair and been recognized, says: "I move that a committee be appointed to draft resolutions expressive of the sense of this meeting on," etc., adding the subject for which the meeting was called. This motion being seconded, the chair states the question and asks: "Are you ready for the question?" If no one rises, he asks: "Of how many shall the committee consist?" If only one number is suggested, he announces that the committee will consist of that number; if several numbers are suggested, he states the different ones and then takes a vote on each, beginning with the largest, until one number is selected. He then inquires: "How shall the committee be appointed?" This is usually decided by amendment. Eventually the motion is put to a vote.

When the committee members are appointed, they should at once retire and agree upon a report, which should be in writing. During their absence, other business may be attended to or the time may be occupied with hearing addresses. Upon their return the chairman of the committee (who is the one first named on the committee and who quite commonly, though not necessarily, is the one who made the motion to appoint the committee) avails himself of the first opportunity to obtain the floor, when he says: "The committee appointed to draft resolutions is prepared to report." The chair tells him the assembly will now hear the report, which is then read by the chairman of the committee and handed to the presiding officer, upon which the committee is dissolved without any action of the assembly.

A member then moves the adoption of the entire report or that "the resolutions be agreed to." The effect, if carried, is to make the resolutions the resolutions of the assembly, just as if the committee had had nothing to do with them. When one of these motions is made, the chairman acts as stated above, when the resolutions were offered by a member. If it is not desired immediately to adopt the resolutions, they can be debated, modified, postponed, and so forth.

When through with the business for which the assembly was convened, or when from any other cause it is desirable to close the meeting, someone moves to adjourn; if the motion is carried and no other time for meeting has been appointed, the chairman says: "The motion is carried; this assembly stands adjourned." Another method by which the meeting may be conducted is set forth in Section 48.

(d) Additional officers. If more officers are required than a chairman and secretary, they can be appointed before introducing the resolutions, in the manner described for those officers; or the assembly can first form a temporary organization in the manner already described, only adding *pro tem,* to the title of the officers, thus: "chairman *pro tem.*" In this latter case, as soon as the secretary pro tem is elected, a committee is appointed to nominate the permanent officers, as in the case of a convention. Frequently the presiding officer is called the president, and sometimes there are several vice-presidents appointed for mere complimentary purposes. The vice-presidents in large formal meetings sit on the platform beside the president; and in his absence, or when he vacates the chair, the first on the list who is present should take the chair.

47. Conventions. A convention is an assembly of delegates. If the members of the assembly have been elected or appointed as members, it becomes necessary to know who are properly members of the assembly and entitled to vote, before the permanent organization is effected. In this case a temporary organization is made, as already described, by the election of a chairman and secretary *pro* *tem,* when the chair announces, "The next business in order is the appointment of a committee on credentials." A motion may then be made covering the entire case, thus: "I move a committee of three on the credentials of members be appointed by the chair, and that the committee report as soon as practicable"; or the motion may include only one of these details, thus: "I move a committee be appointed by the chair on the credentials of members." In either case the chair proceeds as already described in the cases of committees on resolutions.

On the motion to adopt the report of the committee (a main motion), none can vote except those reported by the committee as having proper credentials. The committee, besides reporting a list of members with proper credentials, may report doubtful or contested cases, with recommendations, which the assembly may adopt, or reject, or postpone, and so forth. Only members whose right to their seats is undisputed can vote.

The chair, after the question of credentials is disposed of, at least for the time, announces, "The next business in order is the election of permanent officers of the assembly." Someone then moves the appointment of a committee to nominate the officers, in a form similar to this: "I move a committee of three be appointed by the chair to nominate the permanent officers of this convention." This motion is treated as already explained. When the committee makes its report, someone moves "the report of the committee be accepted and the officers nominated be declared the officers of this convention." This main motion being carried, the chair declares the officers elected and instantly calls the new presiding officer to the chair, and the temporary secretary is at the same time replaced. The convention is now organized for work. Where there is any competition for the offices, it is better the officers be elected by ballot. In this case, when the nominating committee reports, a motion can be made as follows: "I move the convention proceed *to ballot* for its permanent officers"; or, "I move we now proceed to the election, *by ballot*, of the permanent officers of this convention." The constitutions of permanent societies usually provide the officers shall be elected by ballot.

48. Permanent societies.

(a) First meeting. When it is desired to form a permanent society, those interested in it should make sure only the proper persons are invited to be present at a certain time and place. It is not usual, in mass meetings or meetings called to organize a society, to commence until ten or fifteen minutes after the appointed time, when someone steps forward and says: "The meeting will please come to order; I move Mr. A act as chair of this meeting." Someone "seconds the motion." Then the one who made the motion puts it to vote, as already described under an "occasional meeting," and, as in that case, when the chair is elected, he announces, as the first business in order, the election of a secretary.

After the secretary is elected, the chair calls on the member who is most interested in forming the society to state the object of the meeting. When this member rises, he says, "Mr. Chairman." The chair announces his name, then the member proceeds to state the object of the meeting. After his remarks, the chair may call on other members to give their opinions on the subject; and sometimes a particular speaker is suggested by members who wish to hear him. The chairman should observe the wishes of the assembly, and while being careful not to be too strict, he must not permit anyone to occupy too much time and weary the meeting.

When a sufficient time has been spent in this informal way, someone should offer a resolution so definite action can be taken. Those interested in forming the society, if it is to be a large one, should have previously agreed upon what is to be done and be prepared, at the proper time, to offer a suitable resolution, which may be in form similar to this: "*Resolved,* That it is the sense of this meeting that a society for [state the object of the society] should now be formed in this city." This resolution, when seconded and stated by the chair, would be open to debate and treated as previously described. This preliminary motion could have been offered at the commencement of the meeting; and if the meeting is a very large one, this would generally be better than to have the informal discussion.

After this preliminary motion has been voted on or even without waiting for such motion, one like this can be offered: "I move that a committee of five be appointed by the chair to draft bylaws for a society for [here state the object], and that the committee report at an adjourned meeting of this assembly." This main motion can be amended and it is debatable.

When this committee is appointed, the chair may inquire: "Is there any other business to be attended to?" or "What is the further pleasure of the meeting?" When all business is finished, a motion can be made to adjourn to meet at a certain place and time. This motion is a main motion; when seconded and stated by the chair, it is open to debate and amendment. It is usually better to fix the time of the next meeting at an earlier stage of the meeting; and then, when it is desired to close the meeting, move simply "to adjourn," which is a privileged motion and cannot be debated. When this motion is carried, the chair says: "This meeting stands adjourned, to meet at," and so on, specifying the time and place of the next meeting.

(b) Second meeting. At the next meeting the officers of the previous meeting, if present, serve until the permanent officers are elected. When the hour arrives for the meeting, the chairman standing, says, "The meeting will please come to order." As soon as the assembly is seated, he adds, "The secretary will read the minutes of the last meeting." If anyone notices an error in the minutes, he can state the fact as soon as the secretary finishes reading them; if there is no objection, without waiting for a motion, the chair directs the secretary to make the correction. The chair then says, "If there is no objection the minutes will stand approved as read" (or "corrected," if any corrections have been made).

He announces as the next business in order the report of the committee on bylaws. The chairman of the committee, after addressing "Mr. Chairman" and being recognized, reads the committee's report and hands it to the chair. If no motion is made, the chair says, "You have heard the report read. What action shall be taken upon it?" Someone moves its adoption or, still better, moves "the adoption of the bylaws reported by the committee," and the chair says, "The question is on the adoption of the bylaws reported by the committee." He then reads the first article of the bylaws and asks, "Are there any amendments proposed to this article?" If none are offered, after a pause, he reads the next article, asks the same question, and proceeds thus until he reads the last article, when he says, "The bylaws having been read, the document is open to the amendment." Now anyone can move amendments to any part of the bylaws.

When the chair thinks the bylaws have been modified to suit the wishes of the assembly, he inquires: "Are you ready for the question?" If no one wishes to speak, he puts the question, "As many as are in favor will say aye." He distinctly announces the result of the vote. If the articles of the bylaws are subdivided into sections or paragraphs, then the amendments should be made by sections or paragraphs, instead of by articles.

The chair now states that the bylaws having been adopted, it will be necessary for those wishing to become members to sign (and pay the initiation fee, if required by the bylaws), and suggests, if the assembly is a large one, a recess be taken for the purpose. A motion is then made to take a recess for say ten minutes or until the constitution is signed. The bylaws being signed, no one is permitted to vote except those who have signed.

The chairman then asks: "What is the further pleasure of the meeting?" or states that the next business in order is the election of the permanent officers of the society. In either case someone moves the appointment of a committee to nominate the permanent officers of the society, which motion is treated as already described. As each officer is elected, he replaces the temporary one; and when they are all elected, the organization is completed.

(If the society wishes, it could be incorporated according to the laws of the state in which it is situated. For this purpose someone on the committee on the bylaws should consult a lawyer before this second meeting, so that the bylaws may conform to the laws. In this case the directors are usually instructed to take the proper measures to have the society incorporated.)

49. Bylaws and other rules. An organization is bound by external and internal rules. The external ones include requirements of parent organizations and governmental laws, sometimes including the corporate law of the state. (An organization may choose to incorporate itself in a particular state, and in such a case it should consult a lawyer concerning the requirements the state imposes, as mentioned in Section 48.) The internal rules are embodied primarily in the chief document, the bylaws. Some organizations insist on having two chief documents, the constitution and the bylaws; but such a practice is obsolete, inconvenient, and potentially dangerous. There should be only one chief document, normally called bylaws (although it could be called constitution and bylaws—or any other name the organization chooses). Rules of order and standing rules will be treated later in this section.

Bylaws should be drafted by a committee at the beginning of an organization's existence, and that committee should imitate the sample bylaws that appear below, adapting them as needed but always using great care with the language and trying to be realistic in foreseeing changes in the organization as it continues. After the committee has completed its work, it reports to the assembly; and the assembly, after debate and possible amendment, adopts the bylaws by a main motion (requiring a majority vote). It is the secretary's duty to keep an accurate master copy of the bylaws available for examination by all members, and many organizations provide copies for their members.

Bylaws are divided into parts called articles, traditionally with Roman numerals, and the articles are divided into sections, traditionally with Arabic numerals. In some cases, sections are divided into subsections, traditionally with letters. The articles are normally titled; other provisions might or might not be titled. The basic articles of a set of bylaws are those concerning the name, the object(s), the members, the officers, the meetings, the parliamentary authority (that is, a manual of rules, such as this one), and the amending procedure for the document. Some organizations require additional articles, typically concerning a board, committees, finances, or ethics. The bylaws should not contain trivial matters or temporary provisions; they are meant to provide the most basic regulations, understandable by the typical member, and important enough that they will not need to be changed often.

The following sample bylaws show basic provisions for a simple unincorporated organization. After the sample are some additional comments on the various articles in bylaws.

SAMPLE BYLAWS

Bylaws of the ABC Society

ARTICLE I—Name

The name of this organization shall be the ABC Society.

ARTICLE II—Object

The object of the Society shall be to study and express opinions on matters of civic interest.

ARTICLE III—Members

Section 1. Any adult person shall be eligible for membership in the Society and shall become a member upon completion of the Society's application form and payment in advance of an initiation fee and the full amount of annual dues.

Section 2. The initiation fee shall be one hundred dollars.

Section 3. The annual dues shall be fifty dollars and shall be payable on or before July 1 of each year.

Section 4. The treasurer shall notify members delinquent by one month in their dues, and those members shall forfeit membership on August 20 if their dues remain unpaid. Any reinstatement shall be as new members.

ARTICLE IV—Officers

Section 1. The officers of the Society shall be a president, a first vice-president, a second vice-president, a secretary, and a treasurer.

Section 2. The officers shall perform the duties described in the parliamentary authority and these bylaws.

Section 3. The officers shall be elected by ballot at the annual meeting to serve a term of one year and until their successors are elected. Their term of office shall begin upon adjournment of the annual meeting.

Section 4. No person shall hold office if he is not a member, and no member shall hold more than one office at a time.

ARTICLE V—Meetings

Section 1. A regular meeting of the Society shall be held on the first Monday of every month, unless the Society orders otherwise in advance.

Section 2. The regular meeting in January shall be known as the annual meeting and shall be for the purpose of electing officers, receiving annual reports, and conducting any other business that may arise.

Section 3. A special meeting may be held upon the call of the president or on the written request of any twenty members of the Society. The purpose of the meeting shall be set forth in the notice.

Section 4. No notice shall be required for a regular meeting except the annual meeting, which shall require notice of at least twenty-five days. Notice of a special meeting shall be given at least eight days in advance.

Section 5. One fourth of the membership shall constitute a quorum.

ARTICLE VI—Parliamentary Authority

The rules contained in the Modern Edition of *Robert's Rules of Order* shall govern the Society in all cases where they are not inconsistent with these bylaws and any special rules of order the Society may adopt.

ARTICLE VII—Amendment

These bylaws may be amended at any regular or special meeting of the Society by a two-thirds vote, provided that previous notice of the amendment was given to all members at least eight days in advance.

The following comments on bylaw provisions may be helpful in a committee drafting bylaws or anyone preparing amendments to bylaws.

The first article contains the name of the organization, including any abbreviations of that name. It may also refer to parent organizations and establish the relationship between the two organizations, and it may briefly describe the organization, perhaps by saying it is a nonprofit organization. (If the organization is incorporated, this article and the following one may be omitted, because the incorporating papers establish the name and object.)

The second article concerns the object(s) of the organization, and it is typically called "object," "purposes," or "objectives." Although an organization must have an object specific enough to define its membership and maintain interest, the bylaw provisions in this article should be general enough to permit flexibility and growth. The sample bylaws provide a very general purpose.

The third article concerns membership. It should specify conditions for becoming and remaining a member, such as application, dues, and other obligations. If there are to be any obligations, such as possible assessments, they must be authorized by the bylaws. Usually it is advisable to set forth a specific procedure for forfeiture of membership for failure to pay dues after a certain period of time. If there is to be more than one class of membership, this article should so provide. The article may also provide for honorary membership.

The fourth article concerns officers and should specify their titles (in descending order), their duties (either by enumeration, which can be rather lengthy, or by reference to a parliamentary manual), their qualifications, their election, their terms, and, if desired, their removal. Thus, this article often provides more details than the sample shows. For instance, it might give details of the electing procedure, such as the method of nominating. The article may establish a procedure for filling vacancies; if it does not, the organization fills the vacancy in the same manner it filled the office originally, except a vacancy in the office of president is automatically filled by the first vice-president, and the vacancy occurs in the lowest-ranking vice-presidency. Unless the bylaws provide otherwise, notice of filling a vacancy must always be given. The beginning and the end of the term should be clearly defined. Some organizations prefer to specify an officer must be a member or no person shall hold more than one office at the same time. The minimal officers for an organization are a president and a secretary, but most organizations have additional officers.

The fifth article concerns meetings. The first section normally deals with regular meetings, the second with the annual meeting (which is a regular meeting), and the third with special meetings. Remaining sections should establish a quorum and set forth the requirements of notice. It is inappropriate and even dangerous to include an order of business in the bylaws.

The sixth article concerns the parliamentary authority, that is, the manual of rules to govern the organization. It is best to specify a precise edition of a manual or to say "the most recent edition." The wording given in the sample is fairly standard. If it is altered, it should still be clear that the manual governs the organization in general, not just the meetings of the organization.

The final article concerns the amending procedure. If the bylaws are silent on their amendment, they may be amended only by a two-thirds vote with previous notice or by a majority vote of the entire membership. Either more demanding or less demanding requirements may be imposed by the bylaws themselves.

There are additional articles that may reasonably appear in bylaws. In organizations with complex financial dealings, an article on finance may be necessary. In many organizations, articles on committees, a board of directors, and ethics will be necessary. Such articles may be inserted at any logical point, but usually those on boards and committees appear after the article on meetings.

An article on boards authorizes a board by a title, such as board of directors, board of trustees, executive board, and so forth. It then proceeds to specify the membership of the board, its powers, its meetings (including its quorum), and its authority to adopt rules governing its own proceedings. A restrictive provision will say the board "shall have authority over the affairs of the Society between its meetings, shall make recommendations to the Society, shall perform any duties specified elsewhere in the bylaws, and shall act as directed by the Society. No action of the board shall conflict with action taken by the Society." A less restrictive provision, most likely to occur in an organization that rarely meets or is primarily social in nature, would give the board "authority over all affairs of the Society except. . . ."

An article on committees usually refers to the standing committees by name and then allows for special committees to be authorized by the assembly from time tó time. An article on committees may become lengthy, because it is usually necessary to have a separate section giving the duties or areas of interest for each standing committee. Furthermore, it might specify the method of appointing members to the committees. An article on committees will often designate one or more persons as ex-officio members of the committees. Such persons are those who are automatically committee members by virtue of another position that they have, either inside or outside the organization. For instance, the governor of a state or the president of an organization might be made an ex-officio member of some or all committees, though it is usually wise to exclude officers from ex-officio membership on the nominating committee. Ex-officio members of a committee have full rights on that committee, including the right to receive notices and to vote. They are counted in calculating a quorum and in determining if a quorum is present, unless they are from a position outside the organization. (A president who is appointed to a large number of committees by the bylaws is treated as being from outside the organization.)

Bylaws may be amended only as set forth in the description of the amending article above. A motion to amend the bylaws is a type of main motion, specifically one to amend something previously adopted. In the event of a conflict between the procedure for amending the bylaws and the rules governing the motion to amend something previously adopted, however, the former takes priority. A bylaw amendment takes effect immediately upon its adoption, unless it provides otherwise or a different effective time has been set by the previous adoption of an incidental motion to that effect. Extensive bylaw amendments are known as a revision.

Because bylaws are the most important internal document in an organization, containing only permanent provisions, they cannot be suspended unless they provide for their own suspension, and such a provision is very likely to apply only to a specific part of the bylaws.

The secondary internal governing document of an organization is its rules of order. These are the rules contained in the specified parliamentary manual as well as any amendments to that manual. Such amendments are called special rules of order and may be adopted by a two-thirds vote with previous notice or by a vote of a majority of the entire membership without previous notice. If they are to apply only to a single session, they require no notice and only a two-thirds vote for adoption. In either case, such a motion is treated as a main motion except as noted. A typical special rule of order might establish debate limits other than those in the parliamentary manual, either permanently or for a single session.

Special rules of order may be amended after their adoption only by the same rules as those given above for their adoption.

Special rules of order may be suspended by the normal motion to suspend the rules.

The lowest-ranking internal governing document is the standing rules. These rules—which are often not rules in the traditional sense of the term, because they are often not procedural—are simply any adopted main motions of an indefinitely continuing nature, other than bylaws or rules of order. Sometimes standing rules are known by the title of policies, procedures, or a similar term. A motion that people may not wear hats in meetings would be a standing rule. A motion requiring two signatures on any check over a certain amount would be a standing rule. A motion to adopt a budget for a one-year period would *not* be a standing rule because its existence is not indefinite in its term—it expires in one year. A standing rule is adopted in the same manner as a normal main motion.

A standing rule may be amended after its adoption only by the procedure for amending any other adopted motion.

A standing rule may be suspended by the normal motion to suspend the rules, except only a majority vote is required for adoption of such a suspension.

The bylaws, the special rules of order, and the standing rules should be kept together in the care of the secretary.

In the event of a conflict between two or more of the documents, the highest-ranking takes priority; this rule, however, should not be taken to exclude qualifications or details given in the lower-ranking document. For instance, the bylaws might make provision for an election, but the special rules of order might give more details about the procedure for the election, and such rules are not in conflict with the higher-ranking document.

ARTICLE X: OFFICERS AND BOARDS

[Sections 50–53]

———————

50. President and vice-president. The presiding officer, when no other title has been assigned, is ordinarily called the chairman (or in religious assemblies, usually the moderator); almost always, however, a title is assigned to him by the bylaws, and president is the most popular title. A president's most important duty is revealed by his title: to preside over meetings. In many organizations, however, additional duties, usually of an administrative nature, are imposed, but they must be specified in the bylaws.

The following are the duties generally understood to be presidential, whether or not enumerated in the bylaws: to open the meetings at the time they are supposed to open by taking the chair and calling the members to order; to ascertain then and throughout the meeting, though he need not announce, that a quorum is present; to announce the business before the assembly in the correct order; to state and put to vote all motions in order, unless, in his opinion, the wording is not clear enough to permit a statement of the motion; to initiate general consent when appropriate; to assign the floor to members by announcing their names (that is, "recognizing" them); to enforce all rules, including rules of debate; to maintain order and decorum; to respond to parliamentary inquiries, points of order, and any other motions that require action by the chair; to maintain his impartiality; to *try* to alternate between pro and con when conducting debate on a motion; to declare the assembly recessed or adjourned; to have at hand the bylaws, rules of order, standing rules, and other documents to facilitate the transaction of business (such as a roster of all committees and their members); to authenticate by his signature, when necessary, any documents relevant to the assembly; and in general to represent the assembly, declaring its will and obeying its command in all matters and regards.

In the course of presiding, the chair should normally be seated unless such a position would obstruct his view of the members. He should, however, stand when calling a meeting to order, when putting a motion to vote, when explaining his reasons for a ruling, or when declaring a meeting recessed or adjourned.

The presiding officer should refer to himself as "the chair," not using terms such as "I" or "me."

Rules regarding the chair's participation in debate and voting often require some detail.

The chair cannot take part in debate or interrupt members who are not violating a rule. Therefore, the presiding officer must not comment on motions during the course of debate unless he first vacates the chair, although he may respond to factual questions without vacating the chair. If he vacates the chair, he should not return to it until the assembly has disposed of the main motion. A presiding officer should rarely, if ever, vacate the chair to take part in debate, and nothing can justify it in a case where much feeling is shown and there is a liability that there will be difficulty in preserving order. The unfortunate habit many chairmen have of constantly speaking on questions before the assembly, even interrupting the member who has the floor, without vacating the chair, is unjustified and cannot be condemned strongly enough. A person who expects to debate should not accept the chairmanship. Likewise, the presiding officer should vacate the chair if a motion refers to him alone or expresses an opinion regarding him and others. (This rule does not prevent his presiding over an election in which he is a candidate.)

The chairman of an assembly does not vote unless he is a member and the vote is by ballot *or* he is a member and his vote, cast as he intends to cast it, would change the outcome. If the vote is by ballot, he may vote only when the others vote. Thus, if a vote is not by ballot and the original vote is twenty-five in favor and twenty-four against, the motion appears adopted, but the chairman, if a member, may vote in the negative, thus causing a tie, which rejects a motion. As another example, the vote might be twenty-five in favor and the same number against; in such a case, the chairman, if a member, may vote in the affirmative but not in the negative (the motion appears rejected by a tie, but he can change the outcome by an affirmative vote). In the case of a two-thirds vote, he might also be able to vote: for instance, if there are twenty in favor and ten opposed, the motion appears adopted, but he may vote in the negative and thus cause the motion to be rejected. The chairman can never vote twice, once by ballot and once to change the outcome. The chairman should announce the preliminary outcome of the vote, announce his vote, and then announce the final outcome. The chair's right to vote is an option: he is not under obligation to exercise it in any case, unless the bylaws so require.

The presiding officer should not only be familiar with parliamentary rules but also set an example of conformity to such rules. A chairman requires exceptional ability, and most of that ability must be in the nature of controlling, but to control others the chairman must show he can control himself.

But even observance of the rules cannot suffice: the

chairman should exhibit tact and common sense. For instance, whenever a prohibited motion is made, he should, instead of simply ruling it not in order, explain why it is not in order and suggest how the desired object, if known, might be accomplished then or later. Thus, if a member moves to postpone the motion without specifying a time, the chair should explain the difference between the motion to lay on the table and the motion to postpone definitely. Even so, the chair does not have an obligation to coach the members at great length or advise them of strategic options.

In the absence of the president, the vice-president serves in his place, and doing so is his chief duty. When a vice-president is presiding in the absence of the president, he is addressed as president (for example, "Mr. President"). A vice-president may also have additional duties, such as a committee chairmanship, assigned by the bylaws. In the absence of a bylaw provision, however, he is not to be considered an assistant to the president. Some large organizations have more than one vice-president, and such vice-presidents should always be numbered. In the event of a vacancy in the office of president, the first vice-president automatically becomes president (he cannot decline—he *becomes* president), and the second vice-president becomes first vice-president, and so forth, the final vacancy occurring in the lowest-ranking vice-presidency. Of course, the bylaws may provide otherwise.

If the president is going to be absent from a meeting, the vice-president will preside, and the president cannot designate otherwise.

If both the president and the vice-president(s) are absent when a meeting should begin, the secretary conducts an election of a chairman *pro tem* to preside until the arrival of the president or a vice-president or until the assembly elects another chairman *pro tem* or until the adjournment of the session, whichever occurs first.

If the president vacates the chair, the vice-president should assume it; if no vice-president is present, the vacating president should, subject to the approval of the assembly, designate a chairman *pro tem,* who serves until the assembly elects another chairman *pro tem* or until the adjournment of the meeting, whichever occurs first.

If there is to be an office of a president-elect, it must be defined in the bylaws, with its duties and relationships to the vice-president set forth quite clearly.

51. Secretary and the minutes. The officer in charge of minutes (documents recording the proceedings), correspondence, the roll of members, and similar matters is usually called the secretary or clerk. During a meeting, he should be seated near the presiding officer. Bylaws sometimes authorize an assistant secretary or two secretaries: a corresponding secretary and a recording secretary. In the latter case, however, any reading of correspondence at a meeting is done by the *recording* secretary. In some cases, the secretary may have to preside briefly, as explained in the previous section.

The secretary's duties are to record the minutes and keep them in a book, to maintain current, accurate copies of all organizational documents (including the bylaws, rules of order, and standing rules), to file reports (noting their date of presentation and their disposition), to issue written notices of meetings and certain motions, to prepare the agenda for the presiding officer, to maintain a roster of the membership (unless the bylaws assign this duty to the treasurer), to provide and sign *copies* of organizational documents, to make the minutes and organizational documents available to members at reasonable times and places, and to call the roll when required. The secretary should also provide the chair with a list of all committees and their members. Furthermore, the secretary should notify persons of their having been chosen as an officer or a committee member, and he is responsible for providing committees with relevant information from the assembly, such as instructions.

In the absence of the secretary, a secretary *pro tem* should be elected.

In writing the minutes, the secretary should include the following: the date, time, and place of the meeting; the kind of meeting (for example, adjourned regular); the name of the assembly; the fact of the presence of the regular chairman and secretary or, in their absence, the names of their substitutes; whether the minutes of the previous meeting were approved; all main motions in their final form and their status; all oral notices of motions; all points of order and appeals, including the reasons given by the chair; all motions to reconsider; all elections; all numbers or tellers' reports announced by the chair; the roll and the votes of members when a vote was taken by roll call; names of movers of important motions; and the time of adjournment. The secretary should sign the minutes but should not use the expression "respectfully submitted." When the minutes have been approved, the secretary should so note on them; if they are approved with corrections, the corrections should be made.

The minutes should *not* contain the names of seconders of motions, the secretary's opinions on matters, any withdrawn motions, the proceedings in a committee of the whole, or a summary of the remarks of a guest speaker.

When the minutes are to be published outside the organization, they should be published only after approval and should be signed by both the president and the secretary. In such a case, remarks by the leading speakers may be included, but doing so may require that the secretary have at least one assistant.

Minutes frequently have attachments to avoid the task of copying the text of documents into the minutes, but it is also permissible for the secretary to record only a brief summary of a report (except any motions from the report must, of course, be recorded in full, as required above).

The general guideline for determining the content of minutes, except when they are published outside the organization, is they should record what is done by the assembly, not what is said by the members.

SAMPLE MINUTES

A regular meeting of the XYZ Society was called to order at 7:02 P.M. on Thursday, July 16, 1987, at the Society's headquarters at 2400 Oak Street, Anytown. The president was in the chair, and the secretary was present.

The minutes of the June meeting were approved upon motion by Agnes Kennedy.

The treasurer's report was a financial statement with a balance on hand, as of June 30, of $12,345.67.

The building committee reported on minor damage to the building by the recent storm and the necessary repairs in an amount less than the deductible amount of the insurance policy.

The chair announced as unfinished business the motion postponed from the last meeting, "That the Society approve the rental of a booth for sales and information at the county fair." The motion was adopted.

During new business, Gilbert Rego proposed a motion that, after debate and amendment, was adopted: "That we provide labels for a mailing to members by the Red Cross in a procedure in which the Society attaches the labels to envelopes ready for mailing so the members' names and addresses are not revealed to the Red Cross."

A motion by John Carroll "That we obtain advice from an accounting consultant regarding a change of our fiscal year, donations, and other matters concerning bookkeeping, at a cost not to exceed $2,000.00" was referred to the finance committee with instructions to report at the next regular meeting.

After a program concerning drug-related crime in the community, the meeting adjourned at 9:40 P.M.

> [Signature]
> JOHN WONG
> Secretary

When the minutes are to be read at a meeting (and they should be read at the beginning of each meeting, not just at the beginning of each session), the following procedures are in order.

The normal procedure is described in Section 40.

If someone offers a motion to dispense with the reading of the minutes, it should be taken as a motion to lay on the table the implied main motion to approve the minutes. It should be treated as a motion to lay on the table; if it is adopted, however, there should be a motion later at the same meeting to take from the table; and if there is no such motion adopted, the chair should call for the minutes at the next meeting, before the newer minutes.

If someone offers a motion to waive the oral reading of the minutes (or words to that effect), the chair should take it as a motion to suspend the rules and approve the minutes without an oral reading. Such a motion is not in order unless all members have been given copies of the minutes a reasonable time in advance. Such a motion follows the normal rules governing the incidental motion to suspend the rules.

After the minutes have been approved, they may be changed only by a motion to amend an adopted motion.

It is permissible, if an organization meets less often than quarterly, to authorize (by main motion) a committee to approve the minutes on behalf of the assembly. In an annual convention, for instance, it would be futile to get a meaningful approval of the minutes one year after the meeting that they recorded, and it would also be imprudent to fail to act on the minutes for an entire year.

A special meeting should not read or approve minutes; the previous minutes and its own minutes should be approved at the next regular meeting.

An adjourned meeting should read and approve the minutes of the previous meeting before resuming business.

52. Treasurer and other officers. The duties of the chief financial officer, normally called the treasurer, vary in different organizations. In most cases he acts as a banker, merely holding the funds deposited with him and paying them out on the order of the society signed by the secretary. Treasurers tend to report frequently, and the reports are usually mere statements of the amount on hand at the commencement of the period, the sources and amounts of income during the period, the purposes or payees and amounts of the disbursements during the period, and the balance on hand. It should always be remembered the financial report is made for the information of the members. Excessive details are useless to members, who entrust an examination into the details to the auditing committee to see if the report is correct.

When the treasurer presents his report, it should be followed by an announcement by the chair that it is referred to an auditing committee, which will examine the treasurer's books and vouchers from time to time. The auditing committee normally reports only at the annual meeting. It certifies at the bottom of the annual report of

SAMPLE TREASURER'S REPORT

Balance on hand March 1, 1987		$5,098.66
Receipts		
Dues	312.00	
Garage Sale Profits	624.50	
Beverage Sale Profits	42.00	
Total Receipts		978.50
Total		6,077.16
Disbursements		
Rent	200.00	
Stationery	26.50	
Cleaning Service	420.25	
Total Disbursements		646.75
Total		5,430.41
Balance on hand April 1, 1987		$5,430.41

[Signature]
DAVID PETREE
Treasurer

the treasurer that it has examined his accounts and vouchers and has found them correct (or incorrect, as the case may be). It may also offer additional comments. The approval by motion of the auditing committee's report is equivalent to the adoption of a resolution of the society to the effect that the treasurer's annual report is correct. Such approval relieves the treasurer from the responsibility of the past.

Every treasurer should be careful to get a receipt whenever he makes a payment. These receipts should be preserved in regular order, because they are the vouchers for the payments, which must be examined by the auditing committee. Treasurers cannot be too careful in keeping their accounts and transacting their business efficiently, and they should insist upon having their accounts audited from time to time, because by such means any error is detected and may be corrected.

The form of a treasurer's report varies from society to society, depending on the complexity of the financial affairs of the group. On page 119 is a typical unaudited treasurer's report at a regular monthly meeting (not an annual report) in a small society with no investments.

Many organizations have other officers in addition to the president, the vice-president, the secretary, and the treasurer. The officers are any persons whom the bylaws designate as officers, and common additional officers are assistant secretaries, librarians, doorkeepers, and sergeants-at-arms. If there are to be directors, managers, or trustees, they may be designated as officers, but the bylaws should be clear on this point. Being an officer does not require being elected or unpaid; officers can be appointed, and they can be paid. The title "executive director" or "executive secretary" is commonly given to the chief employee of an organization, who is sometimes an officer of the organization. Honorary officers are not officers, but merely persons designated as having an officerial title, and the conferring of such titles must be authorized by the bylaws. (The same rules govern honorary members.)

53. Boards and reports. A board is a group of members, usually small in number, empowered to act for the organization as a whole in certain regards. It must be authorized by the bylaws if it is to exist, and the bylaws should define its title, membership, powers, and other aspects.

The rules governing committees as set forth in Section 29 and elsewhere also apply to boards, which are comparable to standing committees, and the rules governing reports and ex-officio members of the committees also apply to those aspects of boards. Unless the bylaws provide otherwise, a board may elect its own officers, and it is appropriate for the officers of the parent body (the assembly) to serve as the corresponding officers of the board, unless the board determines otherwise.

Although a board cannot delegate its decision-making authority to a portion of its membership (commonly called an executive committee) unless the bylaws so authorize, it can delegate *other* aspects of its authority (such as research) to a portion of its membership (called a committee). When it does so, it must supervise the subordinate body closely to make certain its instructions are being followed, and the subordinate body reports to the board, not to the assembly.

Boards report in the same manner as standing committees do.

Presidents and other officers report often in some societies and seldom (perhaps only annually) in others. When they report, they should do so in the third person, and the report, unless it is very short, should be in writing, signed. Like a committee report, it may end with a recommendation, but the officer should not make a motion to execute that recommendation (any other member may do so). A secretary may report correspondence or other matters; the minutes are not considered a report. A sample report by a treasurer has already been given.

Motions arising out of reports by officers, boards, or committees should be offered promptly after the report has been received, but the assembly may, if it wishes, defer action on them by various subsidiary motions.

ARTICLE XI: RESOLUTIONS

[Section 54]

——————

54. Resolutions. Main motions that are particularly important, long, or complex are called resolutions and tend to be written in a somewhat elaborate manner. Because resolutions are always main motions, they follow the basic rules relating to main motions: they are not in order when another person has the floor, they require a second, they are debatable and amendable, they require a majority vote for adoption, and they are reconsiderable.

A resolution always has one or more *"Resolved"* clauses, and it may have one or more "Whereas" clauses, but there is no rule requiring "Whereas" clauses. The "Whereas" clauses (sometimes called the preamble) precede and present a rationale for the *"Resolved"* clauses. Each clause is separated from the others by a semicolon, and sometimes linking words, such as "and" and "therefore, be it," making the total resolution read smoothly. The name of the organization is sometimes included in the *"Resolved"* clause, preceded by the word "by," immediately after the word *"Resolved."* Because resolutions often express opinions, they are often printed, and when a resolution is printed, the word *"Resolved"* is customarily italicized. Provisions for printing or otherwise executing the resolution may be included in the resolution itself.

A member moves the adoption of a resolution by obtaining the floor when no other motion is pending and saying, "I move the adoption of the following resolution. . . ." He should then read the resolution and provide the chair with a copy. The chair then proceeds to handle the resolution just as he would any other main motion.

The adoption of a resolution includes the adoption of the "Whereas" clauses, and the assembly should be alert to any need to amend the "Whereas" clauses if the *"Resolved"* clauses are amended.

ARTICLE XII: MOTIONS REVIEWED BY THEIR OBJECTS

[Sections 55–63]

---

55. Objects. The object of a motion is a usual purpose for which the motion is offered. Many motions have more than one object, and many objects can be met by more than one motion. The fact that a motion has a specific object does not mean it is not permissible to use that motion for a somewhat different object; thus, these remarks concerning objects do not provide the basis of rules on which the chair can make decisions to declare motions out of order.

There are eight common objects, and the list below shows the motions commonly employed with those objects.

(1) To change
   (a) Amend
   (b) Commit
   (c) Modify a motion
(2) To defer
   (a) Postpone definitely
   (b) Lay on the table
   (c) Commit
(3) To suppress debate
   (a) Order the previous question
   (b) Limit debate
(4) To suppress the motion
   (a) Object to consideration
   (b) Postpone indefinitely

    (c) Lay on the table
(5) To consider again
    (a) Reconsider
    (b) Renew
    (c) Amend after adoption
(6) To correct errors or deal with exceptions
    (a) Point of order
    (b) Appeal
    (c) Call for the orders of the day
    (d) Suspend the rules
(7) To interrupt or end a meeting
    (a) Adjourn
    (b) Recess
(8) Other
    (a) Read papers
    (b) Withdraw a motion
    (c) Raise a question of privilege

56. To change.

(a) Amend. If it is desired to change a motion in any way, the method that should come to mind first is to propose the motion to amend. A person should find the undesired words in the pending motion and then move to amend the motion by striking out those words. If there are other words to be inserted at the same point in their place, the motion to amend may include provision for inserting those words. When the words to be struck out are the entire motion and there are some words to be inserted, the amendment is said to be one of substituting rather than striking out and inserting. If a person cannot find any undesired words in the pending motion but wishes to insert some additional words to give details, impose conditions, or fulfill some other purpose, he may move to amend by inserting as many words as he would like (as

long as they are consecutive). When such an insertion is at the end of the motion, the amendment is called an amendment to *add*.

The chair, not the individual member who moves an amendment, should make clear to the assembly how the motion would read if the amendment were to be adopted, but he should not omit stating which words would be struck out and which inserted.

An amendment can make a motion more or less appealing, and thus it can be used strategically to increase or decrease the likelihood that an amended motion will be adopted. It can even change a motion so much that persons previously favoring the motion may, after amendment, oppose it, and the opposite may also be true.

It is better to amend a motion when it is pending than to wait until it is adopted and then attempt to amend. The latter procedure requires a higher vote, and members will justifiably inquire why the amendment was not introduced earlier. Furthermore, some motions are not amendable after adoption.

(b) Commit. If a main motion is not written well or for some other reason needs extensive change, the best method of changing it is to refer it to a committee. A motion to refer is in order when the main motion is pending, and it may include instructions to focus the attention of the committee on specific problems with the motion and to set a deadline for the committee to report. Of course, the committee cannot actually change the motion; it can, however, study the matter in an unhurried fashion and propose a series of amendments (or one amendment by substitution) for the assembly to adopt to change the motion.

(c) Modify a motion. If a suggestion for change is made before a motion is stated by the chair, the mover may in-

corporate that suggestion into his motion, and the chair will then state the modified motion. If a suggestion for change is made after a motion is stated by the chair, the chair should attempt to process it by general consent; if that fails, the proper course is that a member move an amendment.

57. To defer.

(a) Postpone definitely. If it is desired to defer action upon a motion till a particular time, the proper motion to make is to postpone definitely. The time specified must be adequately certain (not "some future meeting," for instance), and the motion to postpone may be debated and amended, the amendment being to the time. Such an amendment is debatable. In a group that meets at least quarterly, the time cannot be beyond adjournment of the next regular session; in a group that does not meet at least quarterly, the time cannot be beyond adjournment of the present session. Unless specified otherwise, a postponed motion would be announced by the chair during unfinished business at the meeting to which it was postponed.

(b) Lay on the table. Instead of postponing a motion to a certain time, it may be desired to defer it without specifying the time when its consideration will be resumed. In such a case, the proper motion is to lay the question on the table. Such a motion is not debatable. It cannot be amended by the insertion of a specific time or by any other change. If a motion to lay a question on the table is adopted, the question is not considered until a motion to take from the table is adopted. If such a motion is not adopted by the adjournment of the next regular session in a group that meets at least quarterly, the motion laid on the table expires there; if such a motion is not adopted by the adjournment of the present session in a group that

does not meet at least quarterly, the motion laid on the table expires there. Usually, but not always, a motion to take from the table will be made during unfinished business; the chair does not announce on his own initiative that a motion is taken from the table—the adoption of a motion is required to effect such resumed consideration. Sometimes this motion is used to suppress action, as described later.

(c) Commit. It is also possible to defer action, either to a specified time or to an unspecified time, by the motion to commit. Such a motion specifies the committee and may give further details, including a reporting time for the committee to bring the motion back to the assembly, but it may also omit such details. It is debatable, and it is also amendable. The possible amendments may apply to the details, including the time for bringing the motion back to the assembly.

58. To suppress debate.

(a) Order the previous question. While, as a general rule, free debate is allowed upon every motion, there are exceptions, and it is necessary to have methods by which debate can be closed and final action can at once be taken upon a question if sufficient numbers of members wish. To do so, when any debatable or amendable motion is being considered, a member may obtain the floor and move (or demand or call for) the previous question. Such a motion is a motion to prevent further debate and amendment as well as the making of certain motions (to postpone indefinitely, to postpone definitely, to commit). If the motion to order the previous question is adopted by a two-thirds vote (it being an undebatable and unamendable motion itself), debate is closed, further amendment is prohibited, and certain other motions are also prohibited, but it would still be

in order to move to lay the question on the table. The previous question *may* be applied to more than one pending motion: thus, if a main motion and an amendment to it are pending, the motion for the previous question can be applied to both, if the mover specifies; but it would be applied only to the amendment (the immediately pending question) if the mover does not specify.

The wording of this motion, with its reference to "the previous question," is confusing to those not familiar with parliamentary law. Members should think of it as a motion to close debate.

(b) Limit debate. Sometimes, instead of ending debate immediately by ordering the previous question, it is desirable to allow a limited amount of debate. In this case a motion is made to limit debate in some well-defined manner, perhaps by limiting the time allowed for each speech or each speaker, by limiting the number of speeches on each side, or by designating a time when all debate shall cease and the pending question be put to a vote. Like a motion for the previous question, any motion to limit debate applies only to the immediately pending question unless the mover specifies otherwise. A motion to close debate should be taken as a motion to order the previous question. The automatic limits on debate are given in Section 34. Debate limits, whether imposed by a motion to limit debate or by the rules in Section 34, may be extended by a motion to extend debate, which requires a two-thirds vote.

59. To suppress the motion.

(a) Object to the consideration of a question. Sometimes a main motion is introduced that the assembly does not wish to consider at all, perhaps because it is profitless or

because it is of no interest or because it is in some way too dangerous or offensive in light of its minimal merit. For any of these reasons or for others, a member may properly object to the consideration of the motion. This objection is itself a motion, but it does not require a second. It must be made promptly, before there has been *either debate or a subsidiary motion* (Sections 20-25); if it is not made promptly, it is not permitted. Because of these severe time restrictions, the person making the objection to consideration simply rises, addresses the chair, and—without waiting for recognition—says, "I object to the consideration of the question." No reason need be given, and debate is not allowed. The chair asks if the question shall be considered, and a two-thirds vote in the negative sustains the objection and prevents consideration. Only in extreme cases is it likely this motion will be successful.

(b) Postpone indefinitely. When a main motion is pending, a member who seeks to avoid having the motion come to a direct vote may move the motion be postponed indefinitely. Such a motion requires a second and is debatable but not amendable. The debate on the postponement may enter into the merits of the main motion. If the motion to postpone indefinitely is adopted, the main motion cannot be considered in the same session; thus, the motion to postpone indefinitely has the effect of suppressing the main motion by a majority vote without a direct vote on the main motion itself. In many cases, the same effect can be attained more easily by the motion to lay on the table.

(c) Lay on the table. If there is no possibility that, during the remainder of the session, a majority vote will be obtained for taking up a question laid on the table, the quickest way to suppress a main motion is to move to lay it on the table. If a majority vote later takes the question from

the table, however, the suppression was obviously incomplete. Thus, although it is one very common way to suppress a question, it is not perfectly reliable.

60. To consider again.

(a) Reconsider. When a motion has been once adopted or rejected, it is often in order, within certain time limitations, to move to reconsider the vote on the motion. Details of time limitations and motions that cannot be reconsidered are discussed in Section 28. Such a motion can be moved only by a member who voted on the prevailing side. It can be made even when another motion is pending, but it cannot be considered then (its consideration can occur later, after the pending motion has come to a vote). A motion to reconsider a vote on a debatable motion opens to debate the merits of the motion to be reconsidered. The motion to reconsider requires only a majority vote, even if the motion to be reconsidered required a different vote.

If a motion to reconsider is adopted, the chair announces that the question is on the adoption of the motion the assembly has just agreed to reconsider. The original motion is in the same form as it was just before the first vote was taken on its adoption, and it will now be considered again. Thus, debate, amendments, and other measures are in order.

(b) Renew. Renewal of motions is explained in Section 64. It is a more efficient method of proceeding than reconsideration if the original motion was rejected.

(c) Amend after adoption. Amending a motion after it has been adopted is explained in Section 28. Although it does not allow opening the original motion to debate as a whole, it does have the effect of permitting debate on part of it—frequently an important part—and of permitting

change in it at a specified point. Thus, within restrictions, it does permit a second consideration, and it is more direct than a reconsideration.

61. To correct errors or deal with exceptions.

(a) Point of order. It is the chair's duty to enforce rules and preserve decorum and order, but when any member notices a failure to do so—accidentally or otherwise—he should make a point of order. In such cases, the member should rise, address the chair, and—without waiting for recognition—say, "Point of order!" or, "I rise to a point of order." If necessary to get the chair's attention, he may repeat himself. (If the point of order interrupts a person who is speaking, the speaker should take his seat, and his right to speak will be acknowledged after the point of order has been decided.) The chair should direct the member to state his point of order (that is, specify the objectionable action). After hearing the point of order, the chair will rule it is well taken and will correct the error, or the chair will rule that it is not well taken and will explain his reasons.

(b) Appeal. It is the chair's duty to decide on points of order, on interpretation of the rules, and on priority of business, but any member may appeal from such a decision. A member who wishes to appeal rises, addresses the chair, and—without waiting for recognition—says, "I appeal from the decision of the chair." If the appeal is seconded, the chair announces that there has been an appeal. Section 14 explains when an appeal is debatable and when it is not as well as the chair's rights in explaining the reasons for his decision. Eventually, the chair will take a vote on sustaining the decision of the chair (not on sustaining the appeal). After the vote, the chair states the decision of the chair has been sustained or reversed, as the case may be.

(c) Call for the orders of the day. If the assembly has decided by vote on a certain schedule or time for considering one or more motions and the chair is not adhering to consequences of that vote, a member may call for the orders of the day. Such a call is actually a motion, very much like a point of order. In some cases, however, as explained in Section 13, the chair is not required to act with precision on taking up motions established by general orders only. To correct the chair's failure to adhere, a member may rise, address the chair, and—without waiting for recognition—say, "I call for the orders of the day." The chair should acknowledge a valid call (or explain why the call is not valid, if such is the case) and proceed accordingly, as explained in Section 13.

(d) Suspend the rules. Sometimes the best interests of an assembly are served by suspending a particular rule, especially if there is very widespread agreement to do so. In order to suspend the rules, someone makes a motion "to suspend the rules that interfere with," and so forth, stating the object of the suspension. (In some cases, examination will reveal there are actually no rules that interfere with the desired object, and thus no suspension of the rules is necessary.) If this motion, which is neither debatable nor amendable, is adopted by a two-thirds vote, the interfering rules—not all rules of order—are suspended, and the chair proceeds to direct the assembly's attention to the previously specified object. Variations of the motion to suspend the rules are explained in Section 18.

62. To interrupt or end a meeting.

(a) Adjourn. In order to prevent an assembly from being kept in session an unreasonably long time, it is necessary to permit a majority to end a meeting, but it may not interrupt a speaker to do so. An adjournment ends a meet-

ing, and it is explained more fully in Sections 10, 42, and 43.

(b) Recess. A recess is a brief intermission in a meeting, and it permits a majority to provide such an intermission, but it may not interrupt a speaker to do so. The motion to recess is explained in Section 11.

63. Other.

(a) Read papers. To give permission to a member to read papers is seldom necessary, but there is such a motion, and it is explained in Section 16.

(b) Withdraw a motion. Sometimes, upon reflection, it becomes apparent the best way to dispose of a motion is to withdraw it, so it is treated as if it had never been made. Such a withdrawal is permissible, either before or after the motion has been stated by the chair but not after the motion has been put to a vote. To withdraw is explained in Section 17.

(c) Raise a question of privilege. This process concerns matters relating to the rights and benefits of the assembly or one or more of its members. It permits certain matters to interrupt pending business, and it is somewhat subject to abuse. Raising a question of privilege is explained in Section 12.

ARTICLE XIII: MISCELLANEOUS

[Sections 64–66]

---

64. Renewal of motions. Renewal of a motion is proposing substantially the same motion after it has been disposed of in some way (by rejection or otherwise) without being adopted. Of course, an assembly should not have to make the same decision again and again; yet there are also situations in which it will want an additional opportunity to decide. A motion to reconsider will sometimes achieve that object, as will a motion to amend after adoption. In some cases, however, the best way to proceed is simply to renew the motion.

Renewal of a motion is always permitted at a *later* session unless it was postponed to that session and not yet considered, laid on the table and is still there, referred to a committee that has not yet reported it, or placed under a reconsideration that has not been decided or expired. In each of these four cases, an alternative method is available and must be used; renewal is not permitted.

Renewal of a motion at the *same* session is not permitted, but again there are exceptions. These exceptions are based on the assumption that there has been material progress in business or debate that justifies permitting their renewal. Motions renewable at the same session include the motions to commit, to postpone definitely, to limit or extend limits of debate, to order the previous question, to lay on the table, to take from the table, to call for the orders of the day, to recess, and to adjourn. (A vote on a motion to lay on the table, to recess, or to adjourn is not sufficient business to allow renewal of any of these three motions.) The motion to suspend the rules is renewable at another meeting of the same session.

Certainly no main motion, amendment to a given motion, or motion to postpone indefinitely the same main motion can be renewed at the same session.

In deciding whether to permit renewal of a motion, the chair must bear in mind that renewal is defined to refer to "substantially" the same motion; thus, a slightly different wording or even a difference in the time or circumstances may justify allowing a certain motion to come before the assembly. After all, the assembly has several options for dealing with such a motion if it prefers not to consider it.

Nothing in this section should be taken to preclude a motion to reconsider or a motion to amend after adoption.

A withdrawn motion may be proposed again.

65. Prohibition of motions. Motions that are prohibited are commonly said to be "not in order" or "out of order." In specific sections, certain motions have been described as being out of order, especially under certain circumstances. Some general prohibitions exist also, and a knowledge of them is important.

Motions are out of order if they conflict with any of the rules mentioned in Section 49 (including governmental laws, requirements of a parent organization, bylaws, rules of order, and standing rules). Such motions are null and void, even if unanimously adopted.

Motions are also out of order if they present substantially the same question as a motion previously decided at the same session (*see* Section 64) or if they conflict with a motion that has been adopted at any previous time and is still in force (that is, has not been rescinded or reconsidered and rejected).

Likewise, motions are out of order if they conflict with or present substantially the same question as one still within the control of the organization (as in the four possibilities given in the second paragraph of Section 64).

Motions are out of order if they contain language not allowed in debate, except as may be necessary to quote in a motion of a disciplinary nature.

Motions are out of order if they are frivolous, dilatory, or absurd. A motion is frivolous if it is so insignificant it is apparently introduced only for comic purposes. A motion is dilatory if it obstructs the known will of the assembly; for instance, if a voice vote is overwhelmingly affirmative or negative and someone demands a division, the motion for a division may be considered dilatory. A motion is absurd if it does not make sense (perhaps because of missing words or if an affirmative vote would have the same effect as a negative vote).

When the chair rules a motion out of order, he should clearly explain the reason. Furthermore, if he can assist the mover by explaining when or how the motion could be in order, he should do so, but his advice should not go so far as to suggest political strategies. If the chair becomes convinced a certain member is knowingly introducing dilatory motions again and again, he should not recognize the member, but such a course of action should be an extreme one. The chair should not adopt it if he merely suspects dilatory intentions or if he merely wishes to accelerate the proceedings.

66. Disciplinary actions. There are four kinds of offenses that may invoke disciplinary action: offenses by nonmembers present at meetings, offenses by members in meetings, offenses by members not in meetings, and offenses by officers.

Of these, the first presents the fewest difficulties in discipline. A nonmember has no rights at a meeting: he does not have the right to vote, to speak, or even to be present. Thus, if his presence in any way offends the group (normally by being a cause of disorder, interrupting the proceedings), the group, through a motion or by its presiding officer, may require him to cease the offensive behavior or to leave. The group may, for instance, go into executive session, and a member may propose doing so by raising a question of privilege to that effect. Likewise, the presiding officer, in execution of his duty to preserve order and decorum, may have the offending party removed. Either the assembly or the presiding officer may exclude all nonmembers or only selected ones, as necessary. In either case, prudence suggests contacting security forces to do so, but, if necessary, the chair may direct particular members to act as sergeants-at-arms to do so. Such members should be very careful not to use excessive force; they may use only the force necessary to remove the person from the hall, and legal action against excessive force is likely to be taken against the persons applying the force, not against the presiding officer or the organization.

The second case is slightly less simple. If a member commits an offense in a meeting—such as speaking without addressing the chair—the chair should interrupt, perhaps with a tap of the gavel, and correct the member. If the chair does not do so, a member should make a point of order. The process can be repeated if necessary. If the offense is serious or repeated, more severe disciplinary activity may be necessary. The chair, either upon a point of order or upon his own initiative, may, with or without warning, inform the member he is out of order "and will be seated." The chair should then explain the offense and ask the assembly to vote immediately on whether or not to permit the member to resume speaking. If such a procedure proves ineffective or if the offense is particularly grave, the chair may, after repeated warnings, prefer charges against the member.

To do so, the chair addresses the member by name, explains the offense, and specifies the correct course of action for the offender to take (usually silence or an apology). If the offender accepts, the procedure ends there, unless the assembly wishes to continue. If the offender does not accept or if the assembly wishes to continue, any member may immediately move the imposition of a specific penalty, or the chair may ask the assembly what penalty should be imposed. The motion might propose to censure the member, or it might take another approach, perhaps requiring that he leave the hall until he is ready to apologize. The most extreme penalty that the group can impose is expulsion. Any penalty except expulsion can be imposed by a majority vote; expulsion requires a two-thirds vote. A single member can compel a vote on the imposition of any penalty to be by ballot. During consideration of the motion to impose a penalty, the assembly may require the member to leave the hall, but before it does so it should permit him to present a brief defense, if he wishes. Furthermore if the assembly requires him to leave, it should follow the advice about security and sergeants-at-arms given above in connection with non-members.

If members commit offenses outside a meeting, the procedure is rather complex, because the other members were not witnesses to the offenses. Sometimes the bylaws provide a procedure regarding disciplinary actions for offenses outside a meeting, and such a procedure should be followed. In many cases, however, the bylaws are silent, and in such cases the proper procedure is to initiate action by introducing a main motion authorizing an investigating committee. (The motion should not make charges, but only present a problem that merits investigation.) If the motion is adopted, the committee should discreetly conduct a thorough investigation, including a conference with the accused.

At the end of its investigation, the committee should report to the assembly, ending its report either with a main motion exonerating the accused or with a main motion preferring charges (the kind of act or conduct justifying penalty), giving specifications (the particular acts or conduct in which he engaged) for each charge, setting a date, time, and place for a trial meeting, citing the accused to appear, and designating one or more members to represent the committee in the trial, these members to be known as managers for the society. The trial may also be held before a committee instead of the assembly, but that committee should not, of course, be the same as the investigating committee.

If the motion pursuing a trial is adopted, the secretary should notify the accused by registered mail, and such notification should include the charges and specifications as well as a citation to appear at the trial. From the time the accused is notified, all of his rights as a member, except those related to the trial, are suspended.

At the trial, the chair directs the secretary to read the charges and specifications and asks the accused to enter a plea of guilty or not guilty to each of the specifications and each of the charges. If the accused pleads guilty to all charges, the trial moves directly to the penalty phase; otherwise, it continues in its normal course. The managers present arguments, evidence, and witnesses against the accused, and they are not bound by the legal rules of evidence, nor do the witnesses have to be members (although nonmember witnesses should be present only for their testimony, the entire trial being conducted in executive session). Even so, their purpose is not to prosecute the accused but to ascertain the truth, for the society's benefit. The accused, who may be represented by others, should be allowed an opportunity to present a thorough defense. If the accused does not appear, the trial can still occur. After closing arguments, the accused must leave the room.

The members then consider each of the specifications and charges as separate main motions, debatable, amendable, and adoptable by a majority vote. If the accused is found guilty of any charge, the assembly proceeds to determine the penalty, usually upon main motion of the managers. Any penalty may be imposed by a majority vote, except that expulsion requires a two-thirds vote. Upon the demand of any member, the vote on each specification, each charge, and each penalty must be by ballot.

When the matter of the guilt (and any penalty) has been decided, the accused is summoned and informed of the result.

If the trial was held before a committee, the committee should report to the assembly, giving a summary of the relevant information and ending its report with a main motion to exonerate or to impose a certain penalty. Such a motion is debatable, and the accused should be permitted the opportunity to defend himself in the debate. The accused must then leave the room. Like any other main motion, this motion is amendable, and it may be adopted by a majority vote, unless the penalty is expulsion, in which case it requires a two-thirds vote. The assembly cannot impose a penalty greater than that recommended by the committee; if the committee found the accused not guilty, the assembly cannot impose any penalty. After the final vote, the accused should be summoned and informed of the result.

Finally, there is the case of offenses by an officer.

If the bylaws provide that officers shall serve for a certain number of years "or" until their successors are elected, the election of an officer can be rescinded by the ordinary motion to rescind (a debatable motion during which debate can reveal the reasons), and his successor can be elected.

If the bylaws provide that officers shall serve for a certain number of years "and" until their successors are elected, or if they provide for a fixed term (for a certain time without either "or" or "and"), they can be removed from office only by the process described for dealing with offenses by members not in a meeting.

If the offense is by the presiding officer in a meeting (for example, ignoring motions), such severe action as set forth above may not be necessary. Instead, a member should raise a point of order, and the decision of the chair is subject to appeal. If the chair ignores the point of order, a member should move that the assembly censure him, and that motion, if seconded, can be put to a vote by the member, standing in his place, after debate, unless the presiding officer vacates the chair and the vice-president puts the motion to a vote. Unless the occupant of the chair is the regular presiding officer, it is permissible to offer a motion to declare the chair vacant and proceed to the election of a new chairman. If the occupant of the chair is the regular presiding officer and a motion to censure proves an inadequate remedy, the proper course is to rescind the election or to initiate the procedure for investigation, charges, and trial, as explained in connection with offenses by members not in meetings, depending on the wording of the bylaws, as specified above.

INDEX

Motions

The last word in reference.
The first name in reference.

OBERKLEYXFORD

THE OXFORD DESK DICTIONARY
AND THESAURUS: AMERICAN EDITION

The only reference of its kind available in paperback— combines a dictionary and a thesaurus in a single, integrated A-to-Z volume with 150,000 entries, definitions, and synonyms.
__0-425-16008-4/$6.99

Also available— outstanding foreign-language
dictionaries for travelers, students, and businesspeople:

THE OXFORD SPANISH DICTIONARY	0-425-16009-2
THE OXFORD FRENCH DICTIONARY	0-425-16010-6
THE OXFORD GERMAN DICTIONARY	0-425-16011-4
THE OXFORD ITALIAN DICTIONARY	0-425-16012-2
THE OXFORD RUSSIAN DICTIONARY	0-425-16013-0

Prices slightly higher in Canada   **All books $4.99**

Payable in U.S. funds only. No cash/COD accepted. Postage & handling: U.S /CAN. $2.75 for one book, $1.00 for each additional, not to exceed $6.75; Int'l $5.00 for one book, $1.00 each additional We accept Visa, Amex, MC ($10 00 min.), checks ($15.00 fee for returned checks) and money orders. Call 800-788-6262 or 201-933-9292, fax 201-896-8569; refer to ad # 736 (3/99)

Penguin Putnam Inc.   Bill my: ☐ Visa ☐ MasterCard ☐ Amex _____ (expires)
P.O. Box 12289, Dept. B   Card# _____
Newark, NJ 07101-5289
Please allow 4-6 weeks for delivery   Signature _____
Foreign and Canadian delivery 6-8 weeks

Bill to:

Name _____
Address _____ City _____
State/ZIP _____
Daytime Phone # _____

Ship to:

Name _____   Book Total $ _____
Address _____   Applicable Sales Tax $ _____
City _____   Postage & Handling $ _____
State/ZIP _____   Total Amount Due $ _____

This offer subject to change without notice.